THE
HOODOO TAROT
WORKBOOK

"I continue to be a great admirer of Tayannah Lee McQuillar's scholarly and practical work *The Hoodoo Tarot*. This follow-up work, *The Hoodoo Tarot Workbook*, continues to engage the complicated history of Africans in North America and Indigenous communities of the American Southeast. McQuillar finds fruitful data in the interstices and intersections that gave rise to Black American culture, a term that she uses to avoid ascribing all things found in early and contemporary 'African American' culture to Africa. While not diminishing Africa, McQuillar's work calls us to consider the significant Indigenous influences on Black American lifeways that show themselves in Hoodoo/Rootwork/ Conjure traditions and practices. *The Hoodoo Tarot Workbook* challenges readers to take a deeper look at the philosophy, flora, and fauna of the Hoodoo tradition, offering practical suggestions about preparations for rituals as well as directions that readers may choose to engage. This book is a great companion to *The Hoodoo Tarot,* but it is also of great value as a text in itself. Scholars, practitioners, enthusiastic learners, or those who embody all these will love this new text."

STEPHEN C. FINLEY, PH.D.,
ASSOCIATE PROFESSOR, DEPARTMENT OF
RELIGIOUS STUDIES AND AFRICAN AMERICAN STUDIES,
LOUISIANA STATE UNIVERSITY

"Tayannah takes a step ahead on oracle reading with this book. Much more than only providing counsel or fortune advice, the exercises and meditations from *The Hoodoo Tarot Workbook* are powerful tools for self-knowledge and self-growth, no matter which faith the reader practices. She also brings light to the mysteries of leaves and charm magic as well as important lessons on how to create magic in daily life guided by the tarot cards and their wisdom messages. The historical chapters are a must-read, especially because they reveal and reinforce the non-Christian aspects of Hoodoo and its founder practitioners. The illustrated plant dictionary and descriptions of their magic uses are a highlight for all magic lovers, Rootworkers or not. Along with the guide to the plants, the Elder cards' rituals are very interesting and show how Hoodoo and Black America folk magic relates with other diasporic traditions such as Brazilian Umbanda and Jurema."

DIEGO DE OXÓSSI, AUTHOR OF
TRADITIONAL BRAZILIAN BLACK MAGIC
AND *AFRO-BRAZILIAN NUMEROLOGY*

THE
HOODOO TAROT
WORKBOOK

Rootwork,
Rituals, and Divination

TAYANNAH LEE McQUILLAR

Destiny Books
Rochester, Vermont

Destiny Books
One Park Street
Rochester, Vermont 05767
www.DestinyBooks.com

Destiny Books is a division of Inner Traditions International

Cataloging-in-Publication Data for this title is available from the Library of Congress

ISBN 978-1-64411-633-3 (print)
ISBN 978-1-64411-634-0 (ebook)

Printed and bound in India at Replika Press Pvt. Ltd.

10 9 8 7 6 5 4 3 2 1

Text design and layout by Virginia Scott Bowman
This book was typeset in Garamond Premier Pro and Futura Sans with Appareo
used as the display typeface

To send correspondence to the author of this book, mail a first-class letter to the
author c/o Inner Traditions • Bear & Company, One Park Street, Rochester, VT
05767, and we will forward the communication, or contact the author directly at
TayannahLee@gmail.com.

◆ ◆ ◆

This book is dedicated to all The Hoodoo Tarot
*enthusiasts that expressed their love and
appreciation for the deck. I pray that*
The Hoodoo Tarot *continues to provide you
with guidance and comfort for many years to come.
Thank you for your support.*

Contents

🍀 DIVINATION METHODS, DREAM AND OMEN INTERPRETATIONS, AND NEW TAROT SPREADS

————◀◦▶————

Introduction

Why a *Hoodoo Tarot* Companion?

The goal of this book is to provide the reader with a deeper understanding of the concepts, history, themes, and ideas explored in *The Hoodoo Tarot*.

I received an abundance of wonderful feedback from people all around the world who were amazed by the depth and complexity of our tradition, which had been mocked, trivialized, belittled, and ignored for far too long, not only by people outside of the community but also by many Black Americans themselves who had been taught that our spiritual system—known as Hoodoo, Rootwork, and Conjure—and its practitioners are evil or not anywhere near as authentic, powerful, or important as the healing systems and traditions of foreigners.

Now more Black Americans are proud of their Hoodoo heritage and defend their ancestors and themselves against the arrogance, ignorance, condescension, and hatred directed at us and our culture, regardless of whether the abuse or hatred flows from someone with a similar phenotype. That was my stated mission in my first book on the subject, *Rootwork,* and I am proud to have contributed to this renaissance.

That said, I believe there is still a lot more historical and anthropological research to be done regarding the history and development of Hoodoo. At present, the mainstream narrative regarding Rootwork almost always centers on and credits the "old world" (particularly Africa and Europe) while practically ignoring the land and Indigenous

Americans. This is, of course, bizarre to say the least, because millions of Foundational Black Americans have an oral and/or documented history connecting them to one tribe or another via blood or culture.

The denial or marginalization of our elders' directly communicated experiences is not a surprise considering the history of the colony and its brutal enforcement of genocidal theories such as the "one drop rule," which determined that anyone with even a drop of African blood is to be considered solely Black no matter how they look, not to mention the unspoken "lookership" rule that anyone with dark skin and broad features regardless of their actual ancestry were to be considered of African descent by default.

As a result, millions of dark-skinned, broad-featured people from America, Asia, and Europe were denied acknowledgment of who they were. Sadly, this mentality and social norm created by unabashed, sadistic, eugenics-minded fortune hunters and opportunists is still considered completely normal to most people who inhabit the American continent. So, it can hardly be a surprise when "one drop" of African influence (or perceived African influence) in relation to any of "Black" America's cultural artifacts or behavior instantly Africanizes the said artifact or behavior by default.

For example, the only thing considered American about Hoodoo is the use of the American Indian pharmacopoeia. We are told that Africans were in a strange land, so they had to make do with the plants they found here and the ones introduced to this land by Europeans. In other words, the message is that the people who were already here for thousands of years had little to no part in the construction of America's identity as we know it, which is not only ludicrous but also insulting, to say the least. But as offensive as it is, it's not a stupid assumption given the fact that most Americans, regardless of their ancestral origin, know little to nothing about the cultures of the original people of the southern and eastern United States, let alone their spirituality. Many would die if a gun were put to their head and they were asked to name three Indigenous North American deities—even if they can list African or European ones all day long. And because many consciously or subconsciously adopted the early settlers' dismissal of and total disinterest in studying or understanding American Indian history, philosophies, cosmologies, or metaphysics, they make assumptions without any attempt at a thorough investigation via cross-cultural comparisons, and then theories become facts.

Even today, most books about Native American spirituality tend to center on the western tribes (Lakota, Navajo, etc.) and not the Southeastern Woodlands tribes that many Black Americans claim to be connected to through a mutual ancestral history of working the same fields as slaves, indentured servants, and exploited workers, being the slaves or slave owners of Indigenous people, and/or living as neighbors for literally centuries.

The settlers believed that American Indian spirituality was heathenish, nonexistent, and/or just a disorganized mess that consisted of a series of barbaric or superstitious beliefs and incoherent rituals. Therefore, the colonists did not write extensively about American Indian spiritual beliefs or practices. And we cannot forget that the southern/eastern tribes had endured cultural erasure and conversion (by force or by choice) centuries prior to the western tribes. So, naturally, those western nations were able to retain much more of their language and culture to be recorded than southern/eastern ethnic groups.

Be that as it may, there is enough accessible information for everyone to be fully aware in the twenty-first century that the following concepts and customs, determined to be Africanisms in Black American culture, were also believed in and practiced by the Indigenous people of the Southeast prior to the mass arrival of foreigners from around the world between the sixteenth and twentieth centuries:

- Libation
- Ancestor veneration
- Multicropping

This painting, titled *The Flyer* or *The Conjurer* (1585), by John White depicts a "doctor of enchantments" from the territory now known as North Carolina.

- Initiatory scratching/scarification (a.k.a. getting scratched)
- Animal sacrifice
- Permaculture
- Counterclockwise circle dances
- Reincarnation
- Mound agriculture
- Blanket wedding ceremonies
- Waist-bead wearing for healing
- Spirit dolls
- Call and response
- Circle and cross imagery
- Matrifocality/matrilineality
- Oneiromancy (divination through dreams)
- Decoration of graves with shells
- Complex cosmologies
- Food offerings to ancestors
- Bone divination
- Glossolalia (speaking in tongues)
- Special affinity for rivers/river rites
- Diffused monotheism
- Devotion to ancestors
- Decoration of objects with beads and cowrie shells
- Rituals of sacred mediation
- Animation of sacred objects
- Step/stomp dancing
- Spirit possession

Also consider this passage from *The Only Land They Knew* by the late historian J. Leitch Wright Jr.:

Most Africans had been brought up in a patrilineal society. Something that has interested and at times confused scholars is that slaves arriving in the South frequently forgot this aspect of their heritage and became matrilineal. Many facts help to explain this. A minority of the slaves, including some of those coming from West Africa, had been reared in a matrilineal culture, and the instability of the slave family in America enhanced the role of the mother, who was more likely to "stay at home." In time, the White man's law decreed that the child must follow the status of the mother, regardless of her racial background. But the most obvious and probably the most likely reason is the fact that so many Negroes were not Africans but Indians.

Culturally and biologically Native Americans helped to form the modern Negro. When considering the heritage of the American Negro, the Afro-American, the tendency has been to assume that whenever Negro speech, religion and cultural patterns differed from those of Whites, the origins of such distinctions must be found in Africa. There is no denying the logic and in many instances the validity of such explanations. Herskovits and his disciples and the messianic orator Marcus Garvey, who in the twentieth century advocated black nationalism and a back-to-Africa campaign, have pointed this out. Their arguments make sense especially when considering the West Indies. The problem is that the Negroes' West Indian experience in many respects differed from that of the south. Only 5 percent of the Africans transported to the New World came to the southern mainland. . . . All of this means that when one considers the background of the contemporary Negro one must not look only at Whites and Africans but also Indians.

I sincerely hope my work will inspire people to broaden their minds and the scope of their research. In a nutshell, the ultimate objective of *The Hoodoo Tarot Workbook* is to help the reader expand intellectually, emotionally, and spiritually.

In my experience, the only way to do that is to make you a bit uncomfortable, so the exercises and spreads may dive deeper than you might have expected. If, however, you are already familiar with my style then you expect nothing less than a transformative and thought-provoking experience. I highly suggest purchasing a journal to record your answers and insights so they'll be in one place for you to reference later. Now let's get started.

THE SOUL OF HOODOO

Hoodoo Philosophy

Hoodoo (also known as Conjure and Rootwork, as mentioned earlier) is a healing and occult system with a distinct lineage in North America that was developed and practiced by Black Americans.

Hoodoo has mostly been explained and approached solely as a set of random remedies, rituals, and spells, but rarely is it approached as a school of thought. At the core of any ritual, healing practice, or magic, there is a philosophy at work without which nothing would make sense. Because remedies, rituals, and spells have been ubiquitous around the world since time immemorial, it is each culture's philosophical approach that makes their systems unique and sacred.

It is also by understanding the philosophical principle's governing cultural artifacts that scholars might attempt competent cross-cultural studies to discover similarities and differences from other traditions. Unfortunately, Rootwork has not received public recognition as an independent philosophy as it is presented as merely a depthless hodge-podge of beliefs produced by enslaved people.

Though other ethnic groups all over the world have also experienced displacement, genocide, colonialism, widespread miscegenation, the adoption of foreign ideas, and/or violence, no one says that their cultural artifacts are not fundamentally theirs. For example, no one says that Italian or Spanish cuisine is American or African because they include ingredients such as tomatoes, basil, garlic, eggplant, paprika, chili peppers, and so on.

Sadly, that is often not true of Black American cultural artifacts, which are routinely classified as "not ours" even if we're prone to cultural diffusion like everyone else on the planet. That, or our cultural artifacts that other ethnic groups respect or admire are ethnically cleansed and simply become national treasures once they are mimicked by those other groups. It appears the only thing that is ever uniquely "ours" to claim is our trauma and the dysfunctional or toxic behaviors resulting from it.

The result is a failure to recognize our distinctive value in terms of our ways of thinking and being that produced all that we have created. We sacrifice our lineage identity and understanding of our own philosophy for validation and acceptance from those who do not sacrifice their unique lineage identities, no matter where they've settled. In the minds of many Black Americans, it makes sense for them to ignore Rootwork since our spirituality is often seen as intellectually, culturally, and spiritually lacking because of its flexibility, apparent simplicity, and nonbureaucratic nature.

So, what values might be considered fundamental to the philosophy of American Conjure? I can think of five:

1. **Freedom:** No one has the absolute right to determine how an individual should connect with nature or serve God.
2. **Universal power:** Everything in the universe has the power to harm, to heal, or both.
3. **Exclusivity:** A practitioner's most sacred knowledge or powerful tools are reserved for worthy family members or their most trusted students/initiates.
4. **Matrifocality:** Spiritually insightful, wise, experienced older women with a long record of proven service to others are revered and believed to be the spiritual backbone and moral guide of their communities.
5. **Miracle summoning:** It is believed that unpleasant outcomes may be changed with a victory-focused mind-set coupled with the right supplications, remedies, sacrifices, prayers, or rituals.

This list is by no means meant to be a final say on the matter, and I encourage each practitioner to reflect on their philosophical approach to Rootwork.

The Three Sacred Circles

The Medicine Wheel, the Kongo Cosmogram, and Eternal Love

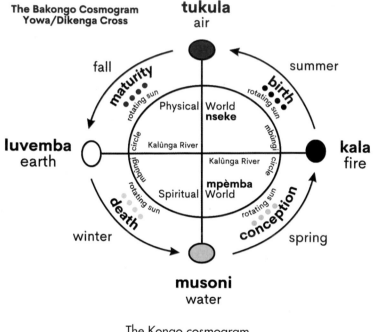

The Kongo cosmogram
MiddleOfAfrica, CC BY-SA 4.0

There are many practitioners of Hoodoo who utilize circle and cross imagery in their workings. This imagery is usually used to designate an object or area as particularly sacred or to remind all those who see it of the cyclical nature of life. This is not a surprise, because all the cultures that have significantly influenced Rootwork have an affinity for sacred

INNER TRADITIONS
BEAR & COMPANY

Inner Traditions • Bear & Company
P.O. Box 388
Rochester, VT 05767-0388
U.S.A.

Affix
Postage
Stamp
Here

PLEASE SEND US THIS CARD TO RECEIVE OUR LATEST CATALOG.

Book in which this card was found _____

☐ Check here if you would like to receive our catalog via e-mail.

Name _____ Company _____

Address _____ Phone _____

City _____ State _____ Zip _____ Country _____

E-mail address _____

Please check the following area(s) of interest to you:

☐ Health   ☐ Self-help   ☐ Science/Nature   ☐ Shamanism
☐ Ancient Mysteries ☐ New Age/Spirituality   ☐ Ethnobotany   ☐ Martial Arts
☐ Spanish Language   ☐ Sexuality/Tantra   ☐ Children   ☐ Teen

Please send a catalog to my friend:

Name _____ Company _____

Address _____ Phone _____

City _____ State _____ Zip _____ Country _____

Order at 1-800-246-8648 • Fax (802) 767-3726

E-mail: customerservice@InnerTraditions.com • Web site: www.InnerTraditions.com

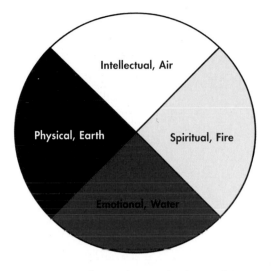

The medicine wheel
Littlejohn657, CC BY SA 4.0, with text added by the author

circles, be it the medicine wheel, the Kongo cosmogram, or the variations of European ringed crosses. The medicine wheel and the Kongo cosmogram are both circles divided into quadrants, flow counterclockwise, and are representations of how these cultures perceive the structure of the universe; each quadrant is associated with seasons of the year, elements, aspects of the cycle of life, and the physical vs. spiritual worlds. Indigenous Americans had counterclockwise circle dances that included stomping, clapping, singing, and shouting and so did Africans.

Many people who find themselves stunned by the similarities between the medicine wheel and the Kongo cosmogram attempt to understand how they became so much alike. The most common theories are that Africans influenced American Indians, or it's all just a coincidence.

The late historian Jack Forbes might have offered a third scenario: Indigenous Americans may have influenced Africans. He stated the following in his book, *Africans and Native Americans:*

The fact of a relatively small but steady American presence in Africa from at least the early 1500s onward may well prove to be a vital area for future research, since one would expect to find Native American cultural influences in regions such as Angola-Zaire and Ghana-Guinea-Cape Verde especially. It is of course, interesting to note that some Africans were already exposed to American cultural influences before leaving Africa.

I have no idea who did or did not influence whom or when, but there are also other similarities between American Indian and Congo spirituality, such as ritual scratching, call-and-response singing, using cowrie shells for protection, throwing bones for divination, and much more. Perhaps one day scholars will think a more in-depth study on these subjects worthwhile, but that is beyond the scope of this book.

The American Indian and African traditions were not the only ones to employ circle symbolism in their practices. Christianity used the circle to represent eternal love. The circle, having no beginning or end, is analogized to God's love for all his children. That's why circles are ever present in Christian iconography in the form of halos in art-work, holiday wreaths, wedding rings, and even rainbows, which represent the covenant God made with Noah. Rainbows are full circles, but unless you're at high altitude, all you see is an arched semicircle. Prior to

Left, pre-Christian sun cross; *right,* ringed cross

Christianity, Europeans used an equilateral cross inside a circle, called a sun cross, which symbolized the sun and its life-giving properties. After Christianity, the sun cross symbolized hope, the light of God, and the resurrection of Jesus Christ. Taking all these examples into account, it's not hard to see how or why Rootworkers perceive the world in a non-linear fashion.

Hoodoo's Holy Spirit

Insights on Early Black American Christianity

Though many Rootworkers claimed assimilation to Judeo-Christian principles, it is clear by their open presence in our communities that they still practiced Hoodoo, and those in the community who didn't share their faith left them alone to do so. There are no reports of forced exile or violence against practitioners based solely on their practice as there were for occultists in other communities. In the rare cases when Rootworkers were attacked, it was because they were suspected of some form of deception against a client or their solutions failed to work. What this tells us is that Black American Christianity was processed and expressed very differently from the Christianity of the dominant culture.

While other ethnic groups emphasized the importance of memorizing the Bible, formal education for clergy, or going strictly "by the book," Black American churches focused on summoning the holy spirit.

The desire for an intellectual understanding of theology was not as strong as the desire to embody the holy spirit. People often forget that the sonic roots of blues, jazz, rock, rap, and all the other genres that Foundational Black Americans gave to the world, were played in church to connect us with divine source. They knew that those entrancing rhythms coupled with a dynamic sermon would create a gateway to facilitate that divine connection.

The holy spirit is unlimited, so anyone present was susceptible to "catching the holy ghost," regardless of who they were, how old they were, or what they were. That which is unlimited is unbiased, so the intense focus on the holy spirit (and matrifocal culture) in Black churches made them far less oppressive than mainstream churches, enabling women and children to express themselves or exhibit their spiritual abilities.

No one was thought to be weird for speaking in tongues, laying on the hands (a.k.a. touch therapy), sharing prophetic messages, or engaging in other such phenomenon. After all, these practices were common among their ancestors, be they American Indians, Africans, and/or Europeans such as the Shaking Quakers who would twirl, roll on the ground, and speak in tongues, not to mention the frequency of these behaviors by the biblical fathers themselves as reported in the Bible.

The emphasis on the holy spirit also permitted pastors, elders, and congregants to be Rootworkers and respected members of the church community simultaneously. And because they were secure with their own cultural viewpoint, they were not concerned about White people's (or even some colored people's) analysis of what they did not understand; their accusations of hypocrisy, heresy, or syncretism; or even the liberties they took in their own interpretation or application of scripture whenever it was convenient for them. There was an instinctive awareness among many practitioners that there were often two gospels that masqueraded as one being proselytized by their detractors. The first was relative to cherry-picked passages from the Bible to validate their prejudice and the second to the Eurocentric gospel of modernity.

After all, it was always the descendants of Europeans who had the privilege to determine who and what was considered civilized, valuable, respectable, acceptable, desperately in need of point-of-view alteration, or worthy of existence. It was as clear as day for those with eyes to see that often it was not the condition of their soul or community that concerned White Christians as much as securing guaranteed submission to their whims and worldview . . . forever.

That fact, that the experienced reality all Negroes faced whether or not they agreed with the old ways, were rich or poor, or were light skinned or dark, could not be denied. The relentless, all-pervasive attempt to fuse the Word of God with the promotion of cultural genocide as auspicious was the "syncretism" few people dared to acknowledge let alone mention publicly.

Today, younger Black Americans continue to leave the church in droves due to a lack of trust in doctrine and church leadership, having other spiritual path options to choose from, and an increased awareness of how our faith was used to manipulate or crush our ancestors. However, there remain many hereditary Rootworkers who still pray, attend church, utilize the imagery, and sing the songs familiar to their tangible bloodline ancestors and who do not share the belief that all things Christian need to be abandoned. They also do not share the perception of Christianity being "the White man's religion," because their families were never sold on the idea that White people, their medicine, their methods, their teachings, or their conclusions were supreme in the first place.

Thus, there is nothing to feel bamboozled about no matter how many did-you-know facts are exposed by whistleblowers or assorted "woke" people on social media. They retain the unwavering faith in the spirit that permeates all things regardless of the fad ideologies of the day and do not impose on those who choose to adopt those ideologies. They simply converse and work among themselves, far away from the eyes and ears of those who are unwilling or unable to understand them.

Discernment, determination, and detachment are how hereditary practitioners helped the tradition survive despite there being a new "it thing" for people to buy into in each generation. Presumably, that is how Rootwork will continue to survive.

GO DEEPER WITH
THE HOODOO TAROT

The Hoodoo Tarot
Bible Quotes and
Why They Were Chosen

As the granddaughter of a Baptist who meditated three times a day on the Word, I am familiar with expressions of biblical origin she used daily. Some were comforting, while others were dark or funny, but they were always thought provoking. In fact, for generations, one chapter and verse in particular was sewn into clothing and used in many other ways to empower and protect our family. Only blood relatives are to be told anything more regarding our knowledge of Bible workings or what we've been told about them.

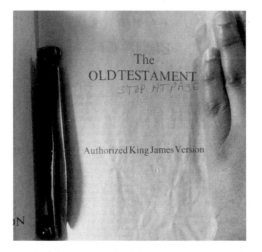

This is the first page of the Bible gifted to me by my maternal grandmother on which she indicates the Bible chapter and verse that empowers our family and protects us from harm.

In the beginning stages of planning *The Hoodoo Tarot*, I debated whether to include Bible quotes, but I was convinced it was the right thing to do after speaking to other Rootworkers. Many of them also had fond memories of their Big Mama's clever use of biblical analogies and metaphors to get their point across, so I decided to keep the tradtion for nostalgia's sake. I am proud that our foremothers were considered the personification of unpretentious, homespun Southern wisdom, and the Bible was usually the thread that wove it all together.

THE FREE MAN

And you will know the truth, and the truth will set you free.
JOHN 8:32

The truth is synonymous with God. Therefore, to know the truth is to be unified with God. The truth may be interpreted as pleasant or unpleasant. The Free Man, however, is free because he has moved beyond the point of preference for the truth to be either. He simply accepts it

BLACK HERMAN

Truly I tell you, if you have faith as small as a mustard seed,
you can say to this mountain, "Move from here to there,"
and it will move. Nothing will be impossible for you.
MATTHEW 17:20

The mustard tree grows from a seed that is approximately one-tenth of an inch. If this tiny seed is properly nurtured, then it may grow to be as large as twenty feet high. Likewise, we can accomplish the seemingly impossible by cultivating our faith.

MISS IDA

Be still and know that I am God.

PSALM 46:10

There are times in life when we feel overwhelmed by the circumstances of life. This psalm requests us to stop worrying, striving, or scheming and trust that no matter how daunting, disappointing, or confusing the challenges we face may seem, they are not greater than divine power. It is the only true source of power and security that no one and nothing can take away from us.

THE BIG QUEEN

Prepare the table, watch in the watchtower, eat, drink: arise, ye princes, and anoint the shield.

ISAIAH 21:5

The message here is to go about your daily tasks but don't forget to make time every day to recenter. The shield in the passage refers to the Roman battle shield that had to be anointed daily with oil for it to remain effective. The shield consisted of thick animal hide and would crack easily if it were neglected, which would inevitably cost the soldier his life. Likewise, a person who fails to replenish their faith and apply divine wisdom daily is just as vulnerable to attack.

JOHN HORSE

Where there is no guidance, a people falls, but in an abundance of counselors there is safety.

PROVERBS 11:14

When people feel they are strong, intelligent, or capable they may become resistant to the advice of wise counsel or instruction. Some may even be so far gone that they feel insulted by the suggestion that they seek aid from those with more experience. The consequence is the loss of precious time and energy reinventing the wheel, which ultimately may cause the entire mission to fail.

BISHOP C. H. MASON

So whoever knows the right thing to do and fails to do it, for him it is sin.

JAMES 4:17

If your intuition tells you that you're heading in the wrong direction but you continue to trek in that direction anyway, you're betraying your divine inner voice.

COURTING

For there are three that testify: the Spirit and the water and the blood; and these three agree.

1 JOHN 5:7–8

When you know something to be true, belief is not only unnecessary but is not even part of the equation. Belief is also unreliable because it may be compromised by clever, corrupted people or our own undisciplined desires. Knowing, however, does not circulate, it penetrates. Those who know the holy spirit require no proof that it exists, for it is as evident to them as water and blood. The right approach need not be debated, because the fruit of right is peace and harmony.

RAILROAD BILL

With God we shall do valiantly; it is he who will tread down our foes.

PSALM 108:13

When someone is truly a person of faith, they will exhibit bravery and confidence when they are opposed, not cowardice. The person who knows and trusts their relationship with the divine never permits thoughts of loss or failure to linger no matter how powerful their enemies appear to be. They remain confident that they will win, which prevents them from becoming negative, hopeless, self-destructive, sluggish, apathetic, or stagnant.

STRENGTH

May you be strengthened with all power, according to his glorious might, for all endurance and patience with joy.

COLOSSIANS 1:11

When times get hard, it feels like the weight of the world is on your shoulders, and you may be tempted to give up. It's when we are facing disaster that we can see how strong we are in our faith. In the meantime, we do the best we can with a positive attitude, knowing that eventually everything will work out.

DR. GRANT

But he [Jesus] would withdraw to desolate places and pray.

LUKE 5:16

The message here is to make time to go out in nature by yourself and reconnect with the divine source as often as possible. Tell your family or friends where you're going so they won't interrupt you out of concern, but plan to keep whatever you hear or realize to yourself sometimes. Nature never announces growth; things just appear when its time. If you experience some sort of breakthrough, you won't have to say a word because it will be seen or felt without any photo shoots, posturing, or prompting.

AUNT CAROLINE

There is a time for everything, and a season for every activity under the heavens.

ECCLESIASTES 3:1

The contemporary world is filled with technology that makes our lives easier, but it can also make life harder if we always expect to be accommodated. For example, in the past people had to wait until the right season to eat their favorite foods, which, if nothing else, made them anticipate the future. Now that people can do pretty much whatever, however, whenever, they require more and more to make them happy. They become frustrated, depressed, angry, or destructive when things don't go their way because they have become accustomed to an on-demand existence. While inconvenience, discomfort, and limitation were just a part of life for our ancestors, now we have a very hard time waiting for relief, pleasure, or opportunities. Our insatiable lust for convenience has diminished our respect and appreciation for nature and natural processes as well. Because it is impossible for us to always be happy as it is contemporarily understood, this must lead people who agree with the times to exist in a state of unparalleled rage, sadness, and disappointment.

DR. BUZZARD

And I will execute great vengeance upon them with furious rebukes; and they shall know that I am the LORD, when I shall lay my vengeance upon them.

EZEKIEL 25:17

This passage was made famous by Samuel Jackson's character, Jules Winthrop, in the movie *Pulp Fiction*. It speaks to the necessity of divine retribution when the righteous have been victimized. There is to be no pity when those who violate the innocent must face the consequences of their actions.

GULLAH JACK

The heart of man plans his way, but the LORD establishes his steps.

PROVERBS 16:9

This proverb is a reminder that no matter how much we sacrifice, how meticulously we plan, or how good our intentions are, there is no guarantee that things will go our way. That doesn't mean we shouldn't try our best, but we must accept that sometimes there is a greater cosmic plan that may take us in an entirely different direction from the one anticipated.

THE ANCESTORS

The eye [that] mocketh at [his] father, and despiseth to obey [his] mother, the ravens of the valley shall pick it out, and the young eagles shall eat it.

PROVERBS 30:17

The message here is that those who dishonor their parents with even so much as a nasty facial expression will meet with misfortune. It is thus implied that those who mock and despise their ancestors won't fare too well either.

FATHER SIMMS

Who gives the ibis wisdom or gives the rooster understanding?

JOB 38:36

The answer is God. God is balanced. To be balanced is to be wise. Wisdom is divine.

MISS ROBINSON

Now the earth was formless and empty, darkness was over the surface of the deep, and the Spirit of God was hovering over the waters.

GENESIS 1:2

This passage was chosen to remind the reader that all things, all people, all perspectives, and all ways originate from the same substance. The worth, value, and desirability that anyone or anything is assigned or not assigned according to our worldview does not change this fact.

THE BIG HOUSE

But the cormorant and the bittern shall possess it; the owl also and the raven shall dwell in it: and he shall stretch out upon it the line of confusion, and the stones of emptiness.

ISAIAH 34:11

This passage reminds the reader that eventually all material things will perish. Sometimes the collapse of civilizations, relationships, or even entire species may be seen years beforehand. Then there are times when everything is destroyed in the blink of an eye.

THE GRANDCHILDREN

Early the next morning Laban kissed his grandchildren and his daughters and blessed them. Then he left and returned home.

GENESIS 31:55

This verse was selected because it reinforces the tenderness of The Grandchildren card. Laban had issues with his son and wasn't the most virtuous man in the world, but he did not forget to bless his family before their journey.

PA

And for the precious fruits brought forth by the sun, and for the precious things put forth by the moon.

DEUTERONOMY 33:14

This message was chosen to remind readers of the equal value of solar lessons and lunar lessons. People may prefer the dark or the light, but they are two sides of the same coin.

BIG MAMA

I am reminded of your sincere faith, a faith that dwelt first in your grandmother Lois and your mother Eunice and now, I am sure, dwells in you as well.

2 TIMOTHY 1:5

I chose this verse because it reminded me of how important it used to be in the Black American community for Big Mama's wisdom to be passed down to the next generation. Especially as it pertained to faith and maintaining the cohesion of the extended family.

DEM BONES

Do not judge by appearances, but judge with right judgment.

JOHN 7:24

This passage was chosen as a reminder to weigh the worth of people and things based on whether they are part of the solution to the ills that plague society and the world or part of the problem. There are many toxic people who are admired and followed by others solely because they are good looking and charming. That is not the way.

THE GARDEN

The LORD will guide you always; he will satisfy your needs
in a sun-scorched land and will strengthen your frame.
You will be like a well-watered garden, like a spring
whose waters never fail.

ISAIAH 58:11

If you allow yourself to be divinely guided, you will find relief, fortification, and everlasting abundance.

⊚ Exercise
Ask yourself, Which *Hoodoo Tarot* Bible quotes resonate most in your life right now and why? Pick four quotes that resonate with you and record your reflections in your journal.

Informed by the Land

The Influence of Nature and the American South

Hoodoo is an American cultural product. The presence of foreign elements and ideas that have been introduced and blended into our beliefs and customs by some practitioners does not change the fact that Rootwork is born from and is informed by the land.

The majority of Foundational Black Americans are inextricably linked to the South by blood and/or centuries of custodianship of the land in the region. Land is central to culture. That's because it contains our history, our values, our ancestral memories, and our lore, which includes the landscapes, plants, and animals our forbearers cherished, harvested, and used to feed and heal us for generations.

The Southeast is especially important. According to the Museum of the Cherokee Indian, more than 75 percent of all medicinal plants known to grow in the United States are found in this region. In fact, botanists refer to the area as the "seed cradle of the continent" because the entire American continent was reseeded by the plants that grew in the southern United States after the last ice age. Also, not many Americans know that the Mobile River Basin in Alabama is one of the richest wildlife habitats in the world and has several rare species not found anywhere else. It is known as North America's Amazon. Sadly, unlike the Amazon, there are no widespread protests, fundraisers, or publicity campaigns to acknowledge the Mobile River Basin as a sacred place or to protect it.

By the 1910s, Black Americans owned 326 billion dollars' worth of acreage (a conservative estimate) in the southeastern United States and lost it all by the end of the twentieth century. Millions of acres were lost or stolen because of biased government agencies, unscrupulous business-men who preyed on the uneducated, and/or threats of violence by racist terrorists. As a result, Black people became more concentrated in urban areas in other U.S. regions as they tried to make a better life for them-selves and their children by starting over. This period is known as the Great Migration. While the West, North, East, or Midwest may have been less hostile, the loss of land was financially devastating as land ownership is the foundation of creating generational wealth.

In addition to the loss of land wealth, the effects on familial bonds and cultural cohesion were equally damaging as they assimilated to the ways of the city and their new neighbors. Without a custodial bond to the land or the sense of place or belonging that naturally comes with land ownership (even if they remained in the South), many Black Americans began to feel disconnected from nature and their unique lin-eage and spirituality.

I can often be found in the mountains meditating, planting native seeds, harvesting plants, or searching creeks for quartz and other sacred minerals.

This disconnect, coupled with the exposure to exotic religions and a wide acceptance of a host of en vogue political ideologies, further exacerbated the problem until Black Americans felt not only alienated from nature or the old ways but also from their very identity as Americans. This is probably the reason why, despite Black Americans' $300 billion consumer expenditures, the focus is rarely on retrieving what they lost, what was stolen from them, or what they were forced to abandon by buying back their ancestral lands in the South or anywhere else in the country.

Perhaps the interest in Rootwork that I inspired with my first book and followed up with *The Hoodoo Tarot* will significantly reignite Black America's interest in their rich cultural and spiritual heritage and a land-based perspective. I also hope my work will encourage people from all over the world to do the same. Earth-based spirituality is impotent and hollow without love and respect for the land beneath one's feet or the nonhuman life that shares the environment with us.

I came across an old Hoodoo woman placing four ears of corn beneath a tree just a few yards away from a tax preparation office. She said she was giving to the Earth so she would get the most out of the tax man. I asked her permission to take this photo.

The Herbs, Plants, and Flowers of *The Hoodoo Tarot*

Each card in *The Hoodoo Tarot* is associated with an herb, plant, or flower (and in some cases a card is associated with two plants). In this section we'll delve into each of those plants, including examples of their current and historic uses. I hope this will provide a starting point for you to incorporate these gifts of the land into your practice; for example, by adding them to a spiritual bath or displaying them in your sacred space. **But always do your own research before using any of the plants mentioned here;** they are powerful spiritually and physically, and **some may interact with medications or be otherwise contraindicated for you.**

Erick Vélez Sánchez, CC BY 4.0

JIMSONWEED
(*Datura stramonium*)
The Free Man

Alternative names: devil's snare, devil's trumpet, thorn apple, Jamestown weed

Native region: Central America

Benefits and Uses

- ☉ Serves as a powerful anesthetic
- ☉ Used for its narcotic effects

SNAKEROOT
(*Ageratina altissima*)
Black Herman

Alternative names: white sanicle, richweed

Native region: North America

Benefits and Uses

- Cures fever
- Alleviates symptoms of menopause
- Relieves soreness and inflammation
- Used to treat a variety of gynecological problems

NEW JERSEY TEA
(*Ceanothus americanus*)
Miss Ida

Alternative names: wild snowball, red root, mountain sweet

Native region: North America

Benefits and Uses

- Relieves coughs and colds
- Used as a soap ingredient
- Used as a red dye

JEZEBEL ROOT
(*Iris hexagona, Iris fulva,* OR *Iris foliosa*)

The Big Queen

Alternative name: Louisiana iris
Native region: North America

Benefits and Uses

- Stimulates appetite
- Cleanses the liver
- Works as a laxative
- Attracts love and wealth
- Used to curse unfaithful men
- Used to dominate men

BALD CYPRESS
(*Taxodium distichum*)

John Horse

Alternative names: southern cypress, swamp cypress, Gulf cypress
Native region: North America

Benefits and Uses

- Stimulates hair growth
- Cures hemorrhoids
- Cures infection
- Improves circulation

D. E. Herman et al., 1996, USDA-NRCS PLANTS Database

EASTERN RED CEDAR
(*Juniperus virginiana*)

Bishop C. H. Mason

Alternative names: red cedar, eastern juniper, red juniper

Native region: North America

Benefits and Uses

- Reduces fever
- Cures coughs and colds
- Used by Southern Indians to cleanse and consecrate spaces and objects and as an incense to amplify prayers

Curtis Clark, CC BY-SA 2.5

WESTERN TANSY MUSTARD
(*Descurainia pinnata*)

Bishop C. H. Mason

Alternative name: pinnate tansy mustard

Native region: North America

Benefits and Uses

- Relieves upset stomach
- Eases toothaches
- Cleanses sores

SQUASH
(*Cucurbita*)
Courting

Alternative names: none

Native region: North America

Benefits and Uses

- Improves eyesight
- Promotes clear, healthy skin

MACA
(*Lepidium meyenii*)
Railroad Bill

Alternative names: maino, ayak chichira, Peruvian ginseng

Native region: South America

Benefits and Uses

- Improves fertility
- Alleviates anxiety
- Increases stamina
- Boosts libido
- Relieves cramps

CHAMOMILE
(*Matricaria chamomilla*)
Strength

Alternative names: German chamomile, wild chamomile

Native region: North America

Benefits and Uses

- Relieves inflammation
- Acts as a relaxant
- Cures insomnia
- Alleviates menstrual symptoms
- Aids liver regeneration
- Relieves arthritis

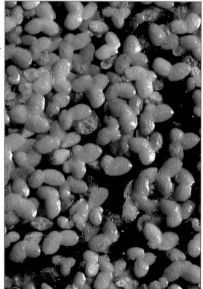

COMMON DUCKWEED
(*Lemna minor*)
Dr. Grant

Alternative name: lesser duckweed

Native region: North America

Benefits and Uses

- Alleviates aching joints
- Cures inflammation
- Liver cleanser
- Induces perspiration

HICKORY
(*Carya* sp.)
Aunt Caroline

Alternative names: bitternut,
    swamp hickory, mockernut
Native region: North America

Benefits and Uses

- Repels bugs effectively
- Sweetens/flavors food
- Reduces bleeding after childbirth
- Used to make hair grease
- Sacred to the Powhatan tribe
  and other Indians; it was
  believed that grits and hickory
  juice were served in the afterlife

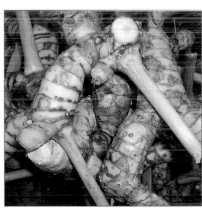

GALANGAL ROOT
(*Alpinia galanga*)
Dr. Buzzard

Alternative names: Little John,
    Chewing John, Low John
Native region: Southeast Asia

Benefits and Uses

- Prevents infection
- Boosts male fertility
- Relieves pain
- Promotes healthy, blemish-free
  skin
- Reduces nausea
- Used in workings to win court
  cases

Cbaile19, public domain

INDIAN HEMP
(*Apocynum cannabinum*)
Gullah Jack

Alternative names: wild cotton, amy root, dogbane

Native region: North America

Benefits and Uses
- Reduces pain
- Relieves asthma
- Cures coughs

Sergio Niebla, CC BY-SA 2.0

FLOWER OF STONE
(*Selaginella lepidophylla*)
Ancestors

Alternative names: Rose of Jericho, resurrection plant, resurrection moss

Native region: North America

Benefits and Uses
- Heals wounds
- Relieves menstrual cramps
- Induces labor
- Treats respiratory disorders
- Removes negative energy from the environment when soaked in water and used as a spray

PEAVINE
(*Lathyrus nevadensis*)
Father Simms

Alternative names: Sierra pea, purple peavine

Native region: North America

Benefits and Uses

- Relieves stomachaches
- Mature seeds are roasted and used as a coffee substitute
- Used in workings to break up couples

BELLADONNA
(*Atropa belladonna*)
Miss Robinson

Alternative names: horsetail, deadly nightshade

Native regions: Europe, North Africa, Western Asia

Benefits and Uses

- Used to treat burns and scratches
- Relaxes muscles
- Acts as an anti-inflammatory
- Cures for motion sickness

liz west, CC BY 2.0

EASTERN HEMLOCK
(*Tsuga canadensis*)
Miss Robinson

Alternative names: Canada hemlock, hemlock spruce

Native region: North America

Benefits and Uses

- ๑ Cures diarrhea
- ๑ Relieves digestive disorders
- ๑ Strengthens immune system
- ๑ Relieves skin irritations

josh jackson, CC BY 2.0

SOUTHERN LIVE OAK
(*Quercus virginiana*)
The Big House

Alternative names: Virginia live oak, bay live oak, scrub live oak

Native region: North America

Benefits and Uses

- ๑ Relieves sore throat
- ๑ Relieves pain when applied topically with whiskey
- ๑ Used to treat depression

SCARLET ROSE MALLOW
(*Hibiscus coccineus*)

The Grandchildren

Alternative names: swamp hibiscus, Texas hibiscus, red hibiscus

Native region: North America

Benefits and Uses

- Increases fertility
- Cures urinary tract infections

MOONFLOWER
(*Ipomoea alba*)

Pa

Alternative names: moonvine, tropical white morning glory

Native region: North America

Benefits and Uses

- Works as a laxative
- Provides headache relief
- Improves reception of messages when scent is inhaled before bed
- Can be eaten as a vegetable
- Acts as an intoxicant
- Used to treat snakebites

SUNFLOWER
(*Helianthus annuus L.*)
Big Mama

Alternative names: common sunflower

Native region: North America

Benefits and Uses

- Seeds sprinkled on graves as an offering to the dead by Indigenous people
- Seeds baked into cornbread by Indigenous people for courage during battle

CAROLINA BUCKTHORN
(*Frangula caroliniana*)
Dem Bones

Alternative names: yellow buckthorn, Indian cherry, yellowwood

Native region: North America

Benefits and Uses

- Relieves nausea
- Works as a laxative
- Heals the liver

COSMOS
(*Cosmos*)
The Garden

Alternative names: cut-leaf cosmos, Mexican aster

Native regions: North America, Central America, South America

Benefits and Uses

- Cures eczema
- Relieves pain
- Used as an anti-inflammatory and treatment for malaria

TOBACCO
(*Nicotiana tabacum*)
Mother of Sticks

Alternative names: fragrant weed

Native regions: North and South America

Benefits and Uses

- Cures headaches
- Stops bleeding
- Relieves pain
- Attracts good luck when smoked with manzanita
- Prevents sickness after childbirth
- Relieves ear- and toothaches
- Sacred to the Cherokee: grown away from other plants and cultivated only by men
- Used as a sedative and antiseptic
- Used for spiritual purification and as an offering to the ancestors

CANADA WILD RYE
(*Elymus canadensis*)
Father of Sticks

Alternative names: Virginia wild rye

Native region: North America

Benefits and Uses

- Stimulates hair growth
- Cleanses kidneys
- Used as a food and intoxicant

FENUGREEK
(*Trigonella foenum-graecum*)
Daughter of Sticks

Alternative names: bird's foot, chandrika, Greek clover

Native regions: Mediterranean, western Asia

Benefits and Uses

- Increases milk production
- Relieves menstrual pain
- Used to treat diabetes

GARLIC
(*Allium tricoccum*)
Daughter of Sticks

Alternative names: wild garlic, ramps, wild leek

Native region: North America

Benefits and Uses

- Aids weight loss
- Promotes heart health
- Aids digestion
- Prevents high blood pressure

BURDOCK
(*Arctium minus*)
Son of Sticks

Alternative names: bardana, beggar's buttons

Native regions: Europe, Asia

Benefits and Uses

- Cures kidney stones
- Promotes healthy skin
- Draws out poison
- Eases the pain if someone's rooted
- Used to treat venereal disease

WORMWOOD
(*Artemisia ludoviciana*)

Mother of Baskets

Alternative names: western mugwort, Louisiana wormwood, white sagebrush

Native region: North America

Benefits and Uses

- ☾ Relieves fever
- ☾ Relieves painful menstrual cramps

VIOLET
(*Viola sororia*)

Father of Baskets

Alternative names: common blue violet, meadow violet

Native region: North America

Benefits and Uses

- ☾ Relieves heart trouble
- ☾ Freshens breath
- ☾ Relieves coughs and colds

Gerry, CC BY-SA 2.0

RED BANEBERRY
(*Actaea rubra*)

Daughter of Baskets

Alternative names: Chinaberry, doll's eye

Native region: North America

Benefits and Uses

- Eases childbirth
- Stops convulsions
- Alleviates itch
- Used to treat STDs in men
- Used to revive someone near death

André ALLIOT, public domain

MAYPOP
(*Passiflora incarnata*)

Son of Baskets

Alternative names: wild passionflower, apricot vine, purple passionflower

Native region: North America

Benefits and Uses

- Aids weight loss
- Alleviates symptoms of menopause
- Relieves stress
- Cures earaches
- Used to treat boils and wounds

Ryan Hodnett, CC BY-SA 4.0

EARLY MEADOW RUE
(*Thalictrum dioicum*)
Mother of Knives

Alternative names: none
Native region: North America

Benefits and Uses

- Repels insects
- Cures head-, tooth-, and earaches
- Relieves pain when steeped in alcohol
- Smoke used to revive unconscious people
- Mixed with mint and used to please God in ancient times (Luke 11:42)

Ohio Dept. Natural Resources, public domain

SLIPPERY ELM
(*Ulmus rubra*)
Father of Knives

Alternative names: Indian elm, gray elm, red elm, moose elm, soft elm
Native region: North America

Benefits and Uses

- Relieves burns
- Eases sore throat
- Mixed with real gunpowder and consumed in preparation for hard labor

YARROW
(*Achillea millefolium*)
Daughter of Knives

Alternative names: nosebleed plant, old man's pepper, devil's nettle

Native region: North America

Benefits and Uses

- Reduces swelling
- Eases labor pains
- Helps liver trouble
- Used to treat bronchitis
- Added to a hair rinse and tea to encourage hair growth

RAGWEED
(*Ambrosia artemisiifolia*)
Son of Knives

Alternative names: annual ragweed, Roman wormwood, low ragweed

Native region: North America

Benefits and Uses

- Relieves insect stings
- Cures toe fungus and other infections
- Alleviates menstrual cramps
- Used to treat pneumonia

Scott Zona, CC BY 2.0

STAR JASMINE
(*Trachelospermum jasminoides*)
Mother of Coins

Alternative name: Confederate
jasmine

Native regions: Eurasia, Africa,
Australasia, Oceania

Benefits and Uses

- Promotes calm and relaxation
- Cures bad moods
- Alleviates chest pains

Vengolis, CC BY-SA 4.0

SESAME
(*Sesamum indicum*)
Father of Coins

Alternative name: benne

Native region: Africa

Benefits and Uses

- Cures diarrhea
- Reduces swelling

WHITE MULBERRY
(*Morus alba*)
Daughter of Coins

Alternative names: common mulberry, silkworm mulberry

Native region: North America

Benefits and Uses
- Heals deep cuts and wounds
- Used as a narcotic
- Seeds worn for spiritual insight

SOUTHERN HONEYSUCKLE
(*Lonicera subspicata*)
Son of Coins

Alternative name: Santa Barbara honeysuckle

Native region: North America

Benefits and Uses
- Cures stomachache
- Relieves constipation
- Maintains urinary tract health
- Used as an eyewash for irritated eyes

WILD BASIL
(*Clinopodium vulgare*)
Ace of Sticks

Alternative name: dog mint
Native region: North America

Benefits and Uses

- Encourages heart health
- Maintains healthy digestive system
- Heals sores and wounds

WILD COMFREY
(*Andersonglossum virginianum*)
Two of Sticks

Alternative name: southern wild comfrey
Native region: North America

Benefits and Uses

- Prevents memory loss
- Cures heartburn
- Relieves itchiness

Peggy Greb, Agricultural Research Service

KUDZU
(*Pueraria montana*)
Three of Sticks

Alternative names: vine that ate the south, Japanese arrowroot

Native region: Japan

Benefits and Uses

- Provides a great source of vitamin C when cooked
- Used in protection workings

Robert H. Mohlenbrock @ USDA-NRCS PLANTS Database, Northeast wetland flora, public domain

PURPLE-STEMMED ANGELICA
(*Angelica atropurpurea*)
Four of Sticks

Alternative names: great angelica, American angelica, high angelica

Native region: North America

Benefits and Uses

- Alleviates menstrual symptoms
- Eases anxiety in women
- Cures colds

Daniel Schwen, CC BY-SA 4.0

EDELWEISS
(*Leontopodium alpinum*)
Five of Sticks

Alternative names: lion's foot, beautiful star, glacier queen

Native region: Europe

Benefits and Uses

- Promotes healthy skin
- Used as protection against evil and a potent love charm

C. T. Johansson, CC BY-SA 3.0

GOAT'S RUE
(*Galega officinalis*)
Six of Sticks

Alternative name: professor weed

Native regions: Europe, Middle East

Benefits and Uses

- Increases breast milk
- Cleanses the liver

ELDERBERRY
(*Sambucus*)
Seven of Sticks

Alternative names: boor tree, elder
Native region: North America

Benefits and Uses
- Promotes immune health
- Reduces swelling
- Used for enemas

POPLAR
(*Populus deltoides*)
Eight of Sticks

Alternative names: eastern cotton-wood, necklace poplar
Native region: North America

Benefits and Uses
- Alleviates backaches
- Purifies the blood
- Cleanses the body after a cold

David J. Stang, CC BY-SA 4.0

PEPPER
(*Capsicum annuum* var. *glabriusculum*)
Nine of Sticks

Alternative names: bird pepper, Indian pepper, turkey pepper

Native region: North America

Benefits and Uses
- Kills germs
- Cures urinary tract issues
- Cures heart diseases

Helen Lowe Metzman, public domain

BAY STARVINE
(*Schisandra glabra*)
Ten of Sticks

Alternative names: climbing magnolia, starvine

Native region: North America

Benefits and Uses
- Maintains health
- Alleviates fibromyalgia

George F. Mayfield, CC BY-SA 2.0

WILD LETTUCE
(Lactuca canadensis)

Ace of Baskets

Alternative names: Canada lettuce, tall lettuce

Native region: North America

Benefits and Uses

- Cures insomnia
- Alleviates anxiety
- Relieves body aches

Alan Schmierer, public domain

YERBA BUENA
(Satureja douglasii)

Two of Baskets

Alternative name: Oregon tea

Native region: North America

Benefits and Uses

- Cures sore throat
- Prevents infection
- Used as a seasoning

QUEEN'S DELIGHT
(*Stillingia sylvatica*)
Two of Baskets

Alternative names: cockup hat, queen's root
Native region: North America

Benefits and Uses

- Purifies the blood
- Prevents liver disease and deterioration
- Alleviates symptoms of STDs
- Eating the boiled root strengthens new mothers after childbirth

SWEETGRASS
(*Hierochloe odorata*)
Three of Baskets

Alternative names: manna grass, Mary's grass, vanilla grass
Native region: North America

Benefits and Uses

- Promotes healthy skin
- Helps women heal after miscarriage
- Used as an incense to spiritually cleanse spaces

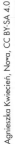

BAY LAUREL
(Laurus nobilis)

Four of Baskets

Alternative names: laurel, tree laurel, sweet bay

Native region: Mediterranean

Benefits and Uses

- Heals wounds
- Alleviates stomach pains
- Cures dry skin

ST. JOHN'S WORT
(Hypericum perforatum)

Five of Baskets

Alternative names: demon chaser, amber, goatweed

Native regions: Europe, Asia, Africa

Benefits and Uses

- Helps pass kidney stones
- Used to treat ulcers and internal injuries

Krzysztof Ziarnek, Kenraiz, CC BY-SA 4.0

SUGARCANE
(*Saccharum officinarum*)
Six of Baskets

Alternative name: noble cane

Native region: Asia

Benefits and Uses

- Fights infection
- Aids healing after dehydration
- Cleanses kidneys

Dick Culbert, CC BY 2.0

GIANT HYSSOP
(*Agastache*)
Seven of Baskets

Alternative name: hummingbird mint

Native region: North America

Benefits and Uses

- Cures cough
- Reduces fever
- Alleviates symptoms of depression

SIBERIAN GINSENG
(*Eleutherococcus senticosus*)

Seven of Baskets

Alternative name: eleuthero

Native region: Asia

Benefits and Uses

- Increases stamina
- Heals wounds
- Alleviates symptoms of menopause

EASTERN PRICKLY PEAR CACTUS
(*Opuntia tunoidea*)

Light of Baskets

Alternative name: Carolina prickly pear cactus

Native region: North America

Benefits and Uses

- Cures hangover
- Aids weight loss
- Reduces inflammation

Sabina Bajracharya, CC BY-SA 4.0

AMERICAN MARIGOLD
(*Tagetes erecta*)
Nine of Baskets

Alternative names: Aztec marigold, African marigold, Mexican marigold

Native regions: North and South America

Benefits and Uses

- ⟲ Heals wounds
- ⟲ Cures colds
- ⟲ Alleviates anxiety

Greg Hume, CC BY-SA 3.0

DANDELION
(*Taxacum officinale*)
Ten of Baskets

Alternative names: lion's tooth, blowball

Native region: North America

Benefits and Uses

- ⟲ Cleanses the blood
- ⟲ Cures stomachache
- ⟲ Promotes general health and well-being

ASHWAGANDHA
(*Withania somnifera*)
Ace of Knives

Alternative names: Indian ginseng, winter cherry

Native regions: Asia, Africa, Middle East

Benefits and Uses

- Relieves stress
- Prevents bone loss and tooth decay
- Relieves pain
- Used as a sedative

BABY'S BREATH
(*Gypsophila paniculata*)
Two of Knives

Alternative names: none

Native regions: Europe, Asia

Benefits and Uses

- Induces vomiting
- Works as a spermicide
- Used to invoke the holy spirit

EUCALYPTUS
(*Eucalyptus globulus* Labill)
Three of Knives

Alternative names: blue gum, Tasmanian blue gum

Native region: Australia

Benefits and Uses

- Prevents and cures infection
- Promotes clarity
- Heals wounds

AMERICAN LICORICE
(*Glycyrrhiza lepidota*)
Four of Knives

Alternative name: wild licorice

Native region: North America

Benefits and Uses

- Cures chest pain caused by cough
- Relieves upset stomach
- Cures diarrhea

W.carter, CC BY-SA 4.0

CORN SILK
(*Stigma maydis*)

Five of Knives

Alternative name: maize silk
Native region: North America

Benefits and Uses

- ☾ Cures bed-wetting
- ☾ Heals bladder infections
- ☾ Prevents vision loss
- ☾ Used to treat fatigue

Magnus Marsæ, CC BY-SA 2.5

JOHN THE CONQUEROR ROOT
(*Ipomoea jalapa*)

Six of Knives

Alternative name: Indian jalapa
Native region: North America

Benefits and Uses

- ☾ Promotes spiritual well-being
- ☾ Cures constipation
- ☾ Promotes gastrointestinal health
- ☾ Prevents conception

Bernard Spragg NZ, public domain

FLOWERING DOGWOOD
(*Cornus florida*)
Seven of Knives

Alternative names: American dogwood, false box, cornelian tree

Native region: North America

Benefits and Uses
- Berries promote men's health and well-being
- Flushes out poisons of any kind
- Purifies the blood
- Cures laryngitis

Doderot, public domain

FLORIDA ANISE
(*Illicium floridanum*)
Eight of Knives

Alternative names: stink bush, purple anise

Native region: North America

Benefits and Uses
- Repels insects
- Stops bacteria growth
- Treats coughs and colds
- Expectorant
- Improves lactation
- Eases menopause symptoms

Fir0002/Flagstaffotos, GFDL v1.2

LAVENDER
(*Lavandula angustifolia*)
Nine of Knives

Alternative name: English lavender

Native regions: Europe, Asia, Africa

Benefits and Uses

- Reduces anxiety
- Relieves headaches
- Alleviates symptoms of depression
- Used to treat insomnia

A. Barra, CC BY-SA 3.0

SMOOTH WILD ROSE
(*Rosa blanda*)
Ten of Knives

Alternative names: prairie rose, Hudson's Bay rose, Labrador rose

Native region: North America

Benefits and Uses

- Restores vitality to infants
- Heals skin abrasions, bites, stings, and rashes
- Used to treat skin infections

POMEGRANATE
(*Punica granatum*)
Ace of Coins

Alternative name: Chinese apple
Native regions: Middle East, Asia

Benefits and Uses
- Fights infection
- Improves athletic performance
- Works as an antibacterial

GIANT KELP
(*Macrocystis pyrifera*)
Two of Coins

Alternative names: none
Native regions: North America,
    South America, Africa,
    Australia, New Zealand

Benefits and Uses
- Loosens phlegm
- Used as a condiment or snack
- Chewed by women who want a male child

VETIVER
(*Chrysopogon zizanioides*)
Three of Coins

Alternative names: khus, botha grass

Native region: India

Benefits and Uses

- Eases joint and muscle pain
- Relieves stress
- Cures headaches

LOBLOLLY PINE
(*Pinus taeda*)
Four of Coins

Alternative names: old field pine, yellow pine

Native region: North America

Benefits and Uses

- Treats sores, boils, and burns
- Acts as a decongestant and fever reducer
- Induces urination
- Used to treat bladder and kidney problems
- Used in spiritual baths for purification

Michel Langeveld, CC BY-SA 4.0

NETTLE
(*Urtica dioica*)
Five of Coins

Alternative names: stinging nettle, common nettle

Native regions: North America, Europe, Asia, Africa

Benefits and Uses

- ☉ Reduces fever
- ☉ Stops swelling
- ☉ Encourages hair growth

Phyzome, CC BY-SA 3.0

WHITE CLOVER
(*Trifolium repens*)
Six of Coins

Alternative names: Dutch clover, ladino clover

Native regions: Europe, Asia

Benefits and Uses

- ☉ Works as a laxative
- ☉ Soothes sore throats
- ☉ Lifts moods
- ☉ Brings good luck

HOBBLEBUSH
(*Viburnum lantanoides*)
Seven of Coins

Alternative names: witch-hobble, moosewood

Native region: North America

Benefits and Uses

- Encourages fertility
- Cleanses the blood
- Used to treat migraines

MILKWEED
(*Asclepias syriaca*)
Eight of Coins

Alternative names: butterfly flower, silkweed, silky swallow-wort

Native region: North America

Benefits and Uses

- Improves the health of the elderly
- Heals sores
- Used to treat spider bites and ringworm

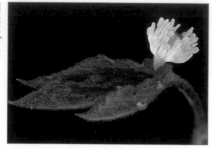

Helen Lowe Metzman, U.S. Geological Survey's Bee Lab

GOLDENSEAL
(*Hydrastis canadensis*)
Nine of Coins

Alternative names: yellow root, Indian dye, yellow puccoon
Native region: North America

Benefits and Uses

- Cleanses the body of toxins and harmful substances
- Protects against tooth infections
- Improves appetite
- Works as an antibiotic
- Wards off negative energy when used as an incense or floor wash
- Used to treat snakebites, ulcers, fevers, sore gums, eye inflammation, skin disorders, urinary tract infections, and yeast infections

Holpaugh, public domain

WILD SARSAPARILLA
(*Aralia nudicaulis*)
Ten of Coins

Alternative names: shot bush, small spikenard, rabbit root
Native region: North America

Benefits and Uses

- Promotes general well-being
- Decreases pain and swelling
- Helps the body to excrete toxins
- Used to treat unhealthy skin

A WORD ON ENVIRONMENTALLY RESPONSIBLE HOODOO

During the colonial era and well into the modern era, colonists and other immigrants transported many species of flora and fauna from their homelands to the United States. Most of the plants included in *The Hoodoo Tarot* are native. What few people were unaware of generations ago was the negative impact that foreign plant gardening would have on wildlife.

Native plants are adapted to specific soil conditions and the climate where they naturally grow. They provide native birds, insects, and other creatures with the nutrition and materials to build the structures they need to thrive. While many foreign plants are gorgeous, the propagation of them en masse by American gardeners has brought many species of native wildlife to the brink of disaster. Fortunately, more people are becoming aware of the problem and are choosing to buy and grow native. This may be challenging, because much of the stock at most major retailers where Americans purchase their plants are foreign.

Luckily, we have Google or plant-identifier apps on our phones now, so we can quickly look up a plant's name and determine its origin prior to purchase. I should also mention that making the decision to plant native doesn't mean you cannot enjoy your foreign plants indoors or in a greenhouse, where they will not affect the ecosystem of your area.

Suggested Rituals
for Each of
the Elders Cards

The Elders cards represent the soul's journey to self-mastery. All journeys are made easier by having clear directions to one's destination. The most enjoyable journeys are the ones for which people have thoroughly prepared, and the spiritual journey is no different. However, there are times when a trip gets detoured or canceled, no matter how much we paid attention to detail during the planning stage. If you've ever been in that situation, I don't have to tell you how disappointing, frustrating, infuriating, or scary that can be.

Once the initial shock of being stuck wears off, people often regret that they decided to embark on the journey and consider going back instead of learning from the experience and moving forward. This section is included to help you work through the issue you're facing.

If you already know the reason you feel blocked, then read the ritual associated with the nature of your problem as described in the introduction to each Elders card. If not, then separate The Elders from the rest of the deck to do a quick one-card spread, asking why you feel the way you do at this point in your journey. Then perform the corresponding ritual—including the prep work—and repeat/reflect on it as needed until you work things out. Remember to write down the answers to the prep-work questions and your reflections on the ritual in your journal, so you can refer to it again at a later date if you wish.

0 THE FREE MAN

O
THE FREE MAN

If you have a general feeling that you are not in control of your destiny, and/or you perceive that external forces are limiting your potential, then this ritual is for you.

◎ Prep Work

1. In your journal, list at least two people who are deceased and who took control of their destiny and/or lived a life that you consider to be free.

2. Record the name of one of the deceased free people at the top of the page and write a brief paragraph explaining why you chose that person as an example of freedom.

3. Create a section titled "Actions" and list what risks they took or obstacles they had to overcome to make them happen. For example, if you chose Martin Luther King Jr., then you may want to write something like "Successfully mobilized millions of people to participate in an economic boycott."

4. Then create a section titled "Beliefs/Thoughts" and list the beliefs they had and the attitude those beliefs inspired in them that propelled them to greatness. If you did not know this individual personally, then ask someone who did. If the person was a celebrity or a historical figure then watch a documentary, borrow their biography from the library, or go online and search for interviews they did that may reveal the information you're seeking.

5. Repeat the same steps for the other deceased person.

6. Reread the "Beliefs/Thoughts" of both people.

7. Ask yourself, Do your spiritual/philosophical/cosmological beliefs inspire the attitude necessary to be free like the people you admire? Answer this question by writing either yes or no in your journal.

If your answer is yes, then you are either unclear about what you really want or you're lazy. That's great! Now that you know for sure that no one and nothing is in the way, you can go on to become the legend you feel you already are. Simply reevaluate your mission or seek help to determine why you lack the motivation to pursue your mission.

If the answer is no, then you must make a conscious choice. You must decide to keep the beliefs that are parenting the thoughts that prevent you from being free as you define it, redefine what freedom means to you, or convert your beliefs.

◎ *The Ritual*

Reread your description of the two free people, the data you collected about them, and your conclusion every time you find yourself feeling unfree to remind yourself of what you should be doing or the changes you should be making to feel free. Record your realizations and results in your journal.

I
BLACK HERMAN

I BLACK HERMAN

If you have a general feeling that you are not where you want to be at this point in life, then this ritual is for you.

◎ *Prep Work*

1. How do you invest your time and energy? Write down in your journal how many hours you spend working, sleeping, preparing meals, scrolling the internet, and so on.

2. Determine whether you really need to spend all that time doing those activities. For example, can you afford to work less or not do so much overtime? Is there anyone else who can take on more domestic chores and responsibilities? Can you wake up one to two hours earlier without sacrificing your health or productivity? How much time would prepping meals on the weekend save?

3. Now that you have at least three to four extra hours a week with which to work, what can you do with that time to achieve at least one of your objectives?

◎ *The Ritual*

On the day of the new moon or the evening before the new moon, write down what you accomplished since the previous new moon. Create a to-do list for the month and a new schedule. Also, make a list of any people, organizations, and so forth that may be able to help you attain your goals faster, if applicable. Black Herman is all about thorough planning and the best use of resources (human and otherwise) to get the job done. Do this every month until you've reached your goals.

II MISS IDA

If you find it difficult to trust yourself or listen to your intuition, then this ritual is for you.

◎ *Prep Work*

1. What characteristics does a person have to have or who do they have to be for you to trust them? Some examples might be honesty, reliability, and consistency.

2. Do you have these characteristics, or are you often dishonest, inconsistent, selfish, prone to exaggeration, and so on? If the latter, it would make sense that you wouldn't trust yourself because no one else can.

3. Were you taught (directly or indirectly) that there are people or institutions that you should always trust even if your intuition tells you not to? Who or what are they?

4. Purchase a book or google a website that has at least one hundred philosophical questions that will encourage you to examine your worldview. I like the Science of People website's list of philosophical questions.

◎ *The Ritual*

Every full moon, put aside some time to answer at least two of the philosophical questions you discovered in step 4. Resist the urge to reference what your parents, your friends, society, or the "experts" would say or would want you to say. Resist the urge to "correct" yourself and just jot down how you genuinely feel. This may be very difficult at first, but it will help you get more in tune with existence as you perceive it through *your* eyes.

III THE BIG QUEEN

If you feel stuck, dissatisfied, or bored, but you can't quite put your finger on what's wrong, then this ritual is for you.

◎ *Prep Work*

1. What nurtured you as a child? What games or other activities brought you tremendous joy back then? What did you dream of being, doing, or becoming? What did you create on a regular basis? Answer these questions as thoroughly as possible. No detail is too small or insignificant. Life's joys can all be found in creation. That's why people tend to feel the blahs when they are not in the process of working toward or creating something that truly matters to them.

2. Review your answers to question 1 and brainstorm ideas of how you can consistently incorporate your interests into your daily or monthly routine.

3. Research in person or online events or courses related to your passion.

4. Research individuals, podcasts, and organizations that are currently influential in your fields of interest and begin following them on social media. In the case of organizations, explore membership options.

5. Do a search to see if there are any group chats related to your interest that you find interesting and join them. Try to make at least one new friend in each group who is super passionate and knowledgeable about the subject.

◎ *The Ritual*

Every month, participate in some activity related to your passion and/or create something new. Make a note on a calendar of what you've done and when so that at the end of the year you will have documented proof of your progress.

IV JOHN HORSE

If you feel that being more assertive or a more effective leader would improve your life, then this ritual is for you.

◎ *Prep Work*

1. List the qualities of an effective leader.
2. Determine from 1–10 how you rate regarding each of the qualities you listed.
3. List everyday opportunities that may give you a chance to practice strengthening the qualities you lack. For example, you may believe effective leaders express their gratitude for their subordinates' hard work or loyalty, but you rarely if ever *show* and *prove* that via your actions to your children, employees, or students. Think of tangible ways to do so consistently from this point on.

◎ *The Ritual*

Keep a detailed log—either in your journal or someplace separate—of every time you go outside of your comfort zone and assert yourself or exhibit the leadership qualities you are weakest at. After every tenth success, celebrate by giving yourself a reward for pushing through despite how awkward, anxious, or terrified you felt.

V
BISHOP C. H. MASON

V BISHOP C. H. MASON

If you lack a clear spiritual direction or practice, and you feel like your life would improve by having one, then this ritual is for you.

◎ *Prep Work*

1. In *one* sentence, what is your ultimate objective for being spiritual in the first place? What are you trying to learn, realize, gain, or attain? For example, Christians are trying to attain entry to heaven. Failure to be able to succinctly answer this question has led many "spiritual but not religious" people to waste precious time, money, and energy on practices, workshops, teachers, groups, products, and so on that are cool but have nothing to do with what they want to accomplish.

2. List four rites, rituals, or holy days/holidays from the tradition you grew up in that you enjoyed the most. Why are they your favorites? What do they symbolize? If you did not grow up in a spiritual or religious tradition or do not celebrate Thanksgiving, Christmas, or other holidays, skip to step 5.

3. List four rites, rituals, or holy days/holidays from a foreign tradition that you respect.

4. On a calendar mark all the days throughout the year that would be special or holy days for you.

5. Write prayers, create activities, or design rituals for your holidays. Don't forget to keep your responses to question 1 in mind as you compose and construct, so you remain focused on the bottom line.

◎ *The Ritual*

Perform your personalized spiritual activities on their allotted dates. Afterward, take note of the things that aren't working and what you can do next month or year to make them more effective.

VI COURTING

If you are having difficulty making a potentially life-changing decision, then this ritual is for you.

◎ *Prep Work*

1. List the potential pros and cons of all the possibilities you are considering in the decision(s) you need to make.
2. List the ways each possibility could have a positive and/or negative long-term effect on the people closest to you (children, partner, and so on.)
3. How could each possibility clash with your beliefs, philosophical outlook on life, or any other core values?

ⓐ *The Ritual*

Right before bed clean your eyes, ears, heart, and feet with sage water or any other clarifying herb of your choice. It will symbolize seeing, hearing, knowing, and going in the right direction. Pray for guidance every night as you're falling asleep until the question is resolved.

VII
RAILROAD BILL

VIII
STRENGTH

VII RAILROAD BILL AND VIII STRENGTH

If you're lacking strength, ambition, get-up-and-go, or a victory mind-set, then this ritual is for you.

◎ Prep Work

1. If you have a natal astrology chart, find out your Mars sign. (If you don't have a natal chart, then you can pull up one for free on the Astrodienst website.) Mars rules our drive and passions.
2. Make a list of colors, herbs, numbers, and crystals associated with your Mars sign.
3. Find out when the moon will be in your Mars sign by either purchasing an astrological calendar or searching for an almanac online.

◎ The Ritual

Prepare a spiritual bath that includes one or more of the herbs associated with your Mars sign and wash with it after you've completed your normal bathing routine. This should be done for seven consecutive days before the moon is in your Mars sign. Smile as you imagine all your insecurities, doubts, and any obstacles going down the drain. Visualize what victory will look, sound, and feel like.

On the two to three days the moon is in your Mars sign, light an appropriately colored candle while contemplating strategies for success and next moves. Keep burning the candle until it's gone, and try to wear your Mars sign's corresponding colors or minerals to maintain focus and keep up that winner's attitude.

IX
DR. GRANT

IX DR. GRANT

If you've been feeling like the weight of the world is on your shoulders, and you need some peace, then this ritual is for you.

◎ Prep Work

1. Consider how much time you spend contemplating other people's affairs rather than focusing on attaining your dreams and goals. How much time do you spend considering the needs of others? Gossiping about others? Reading the news? Engaging in emotionally charged and draining debates online? If you'd like, record you thoughts on this in your journal, then compare your answer with step 2.

2. How much time do you spend contemplating your needs, praying or meditating, or practicing self-care (working out, soaking your feet, going for a night out with friends, spending time in nature, etc.)?

◎ The Ritual

Spend at least thirty minutes or more per day on self-care. Preferably alone. Stay off social media and don't check any emails. Inform anyone who might worry about you that you're okay before you begin so you can focus completely on you.

X AUNT CAROLINE

If thinking about the future is anxiety producing, then this ritual is for you.

◎ *Prep Work*

1. What four things do you fear the most about the future? What would be the worst possible fate?

2. In what practical ways are you already trying to prevent the fate you fear. For example, if you fear being frail and sick when you get older, are you eating right and working out most of the time *today?*

3. Brainstorm ideas and/or do some research on what you can do to avoid the possible fate you fear.

◎ *The Ritual*

Choose or compose a prayer, quote, or song that inspires feelings of comfort, protection, positivity, or safety. Say it or sing it every morning before you start the day or whenever your fear of the future takes hold.

XI DR. BUZZARD

If you feel angry or resentful toward an individual, an institution, or society in general for being unfair, then this ritual is for you.

◎ *Prep Work*

1. Make a list of all your grievances.

2. Make a check next to each grievance for which you have been complicit in the situation. Hold yourself accountable for what went wrong. Be honest about your role.

3. If you were complicit, write a paragraph or two stating how you could have done things differently and how you plan to do things differently in the future. For example, if a store manager refused to help you after a confrontation with a rude associate and you knocked over a display in frustration, first acknowledge that your response was unacceptable. Then vow that the next time something similar happens you will report the poor customer service to the owner or the Better Business Bureau and/or file a complaint with the local consumer protection agency. Then never patronize their business again for any reason unless you are given an apology or are justly compensated for the insult.

4. If you realize that you were not complicit, write a petition for change to your God/gods, ancestors, spirit guides, Mother Earth, and so on detailing how you've been used, abused, or exploited. Write the petition on biodegradable paper in pencil.

◎ The Ritual

If you were complicit in a nasty outcome to a situation, reread aloud the paragraph you wrote. Feel whatever feelings come bubbling to the surface, then take a deep breath and rip it up. After that, take a spiritual bath with sea salt and wash away the negativity that situation has brought into your life. Imagine all the drama going down the drain. You know what you plan to do should a similar situation occur in the future, so let it go.

If you were not complicit in the creation or escalation of an offensive situation, then take the paper with your petition for justice somewhere out in nature at a time when there is no one else around. It could be a wooded area, a stream, or anywhere you prefer.

Read your petition out loud and then bury it or submerge it in the water. Do this on the anniversary of the offense, every equinox, and/or whenever the moon is in Libra until justice has been served. If you know people that feel the same way, then plan to do this ritual together whenever possible. This does not have to be a solemn occasion; feel free to celebrate your anticipated victory!

XII
GULLAH JACK

XII GULLAH JACK

If you have a goal that feels almost impossible or unattainable, and it's bringing you down, then this ritual is for you.

◎ Prep Work

1. Write down your goal in one sentence.
2. Write down *everything* you're willing to do or sacrifice to get it. Keep it real, don't be shy!
3. Draw up a contract with yourself detailing what is to be done and by when on biodegradable paper.

◎ The Ritual

During the new moon, go to a wooded area and find a tree stump. Fold the contract four times, and bury it near the root. Leave the area without looking back.

XIII
ANCESTORS

XIII ANCESTORS

If you don't feel as connected to your tangible bloodline ancestors as you think you should be, then this ritual is for you.

◎ Prep Work

1. What were you told about your ancestors by your family? Who were your ancestors and where were they from? What ethnic groups, countries, states, village names, and so on do you know about?
2. Do you feel ashamed, angry, or indifferent toward your tangible bloodline ancestors? Do you feel they were not enough

in some way? Do you wish they were someone else, from somewhere else, or that they had made different choices? Please be honest and write down why you feel this way.

3. If your negative feelings lie with certain deceased individuals or a specific branch of your family, write down each of their toxic traits in one word. Then write down an antonym for each word.

4. Do you feel superior to your tangible bloodline ancestors morally, culturally, spiritually, intellectually, or in any other way? If so, why? How did you come to that conclusion? What is the proof of your superiority?

5. Consider how these feelings may have directly affected your self-esteem, your relationship with your living family members, and/or your lifestyle choices.

◎ The Ritual

1. Take the list of antonyms you made in step 3 above and brainstorm tangible ways you can model that behavior. If you have children, think of activities you can do together that reflect the positive new direction you're taking the family in. For example, if there is a history of criminality in the family, then you may want to avoid friends, lovers, music, TV shows, or any other forms of media that glorify a criminal lifestyle and replace them with more wholesome choices.

    Stop hating and simultaneously participating and celebrating whatever you consider the problem. Especially around the children. Consider the decision to cut off people who are still in that space along with abstinence from counterproductive programming offerings to your healthy ancestors and your descendants, if applicable. Light a candle in honor of both after you've cleaned house.

2. Get a blank notebook (or use your journal) and write "The Beauty of My Ancestors" on the cover. In that notebook, jot down at least four new positive facts (e.g., worthy accomplishments, artistic endeavors, cuisine, inventions, etc.) you've learned about your ethnic groups' heritage and/ or the land they called home. For example, if your ancestors were from a small town in Arkansas, look up cool or interesting facts about that town or the state itself. What did people create there? Who or what are the locals

most proud of? What are its most beautiful geographical features, animals, flora, fauna, and so on? Do this exercise for all the branches of the family you know little to nothing about.

3. Once a month, watch documentaries or attend events that celebrate the beauty or cultural products of your tangible bloodline ancestors. Especially, if you know nothing about or feel you hate that part of your ancestry. Don't allow your disgust with two, ten, or even one hundred problematic individuals to cut you off from the ancestors on that side who care about you, not to mention the thousands of years of history and culture that are still *yours* and a part of *you*.

XIV
FATHER SIMMS

XIV FATHER SIMMS

If you've been asked to compromise about something, and you're not sure what to do, then this ritual is for you.

◎ Prep Work

1. List what is at stake if you compromise and what is at stake if you don't.
2. Have you consulted a professional for advice or discussed the matter with anyone who has gone through something similar?
3. Which decision is best for the good of all in the long term?

◎ The Ritual

On each of the three nights before the full moon, pray for clarity over a glass of water, then leave the water beside your bed. Take note of any dreams or odd happenings. On the evening of the full moon, commit to a final decision either way. Then wash the bottom of the shoes you wear often, knowing you have made the right choice.

XV MISS ROBINSON

If you feel heavy because of negative thoughts, people, or situations, then this ritual is for you.

◎ Prep Work

1. In your journal, list all the negative people or situations in your life.
2. Beside each person or situation, write down the possible physical, emotional, financial, or spiritual consequences of allowing these people or situations to perpetuate.
3. Are you ready, willing, and able to endure the consequences of remaining bound? Answer honestly, or you'll only be fooling yourself. Write your answer in your journal.

◎ The Ritual

At noon during a waxing moon, sit outside in direct sunlight and read your responses to the questions out loud. Sit for a minute with the sun on your face and make a choice to either endure or remove the negative people and situations.

If you have chosen to release them, face the sun and say it out loud. Repeat "I release them" until you feel it deep down in your soul. Let laughter or tears come if that's how you feel. Then say, "I will see the right signs and hear the right voices, and I will be divinely guided to make the right choices on this matter from this point on." Repeat the affirmation until your intuition tells you to stop.

If you have decided to continue to reserve space in your life for the drama associated with negative people or situations despite the possible physical, emotional, financial, or spiritual consequences, say that out loud. Then say, "I accept my choice and everything that may come with it."

XVI THE BIG HOUSE

If a major life change has left you feeling shell-shocked, then this ritual is for you.

◎ *Prep Work*

1. In what ways does this change make you feel vulnerable, frightened, or alone?
2. Is there anyone you can lean on for support during this difficult time? Have you searched for online communities for support? Have you looked up any organizations in your area or community resources for people in your situation?
3. What do you fear most because of this change? What will you need to feel secure again?

◎ *The Ritual*

Bathe in chamomile and drink chamomile tea before meditating or praying for divine guidance, protection, and the best possible outcome. Do this for seven days or until you feel better. Remember, the calmest part of a hurricane is in the eye of the storm.

XVII THE GRANDCHILDREN

If you are in desperate need of a blessing or want to be consistently blessed, then this ritual is for you.

◎ *Prep Work*

1. If you have a natal astrology chart, find out your Jupiter sign. (If you don't have a natal chart, then you can pull up one for free on the Astrodienst website.) Jupiter is the planet of wealth, luck, generosity, and success.

2. Research the meaning of your Jupiter sign and identify the keynotes, symbols, people, colors, metals, and so on associated with that zodiac sign.

◎ *The Ritual*

When the sun or moon is in your Jupiter sign, give an offering of light, a prayer, your time, money, gifts, or a donation to whomever or whatever that sign represents. For example, Capricorn rules the elderly, the sick, the poor, hospitals, and prisons. If your Jupiter is in Capricorn, perhaps you can do something to make the old folks in your family happier or more comfortable, volunteer at a soup kitchen, or donate to your local hospice. Do this consistently for at least four months, and you should see major improvements in your life.

XVIII
PA

XVIII PA

If you feel that someone is keeping secrets from you, and you want to know what's going on, then this ritual is for you.

◎ *Prep Work*

1. Write down why you suspect this person or people of deception.
2. What is at stake emotionally, financially, physically, and so forth if you discover your intuition is on point?
3. Are you really prepared to know the truth? Be honest. (If not, then please stop now.)
4. What are you going to do if your suspicions are correct? What are the consequences? Do you have a well-thought-out plan of action from this point on, or do you just plan to be sad or mad about it? (If the answer is the latter, then please stop now, or you might say or do something you might regret later!)
5. Search online for an image of a mask that's ugly, smug, expressionless,

or whatever you feel fits the situation. Size it down until it's about the size of your thumb. We will be performing the ritual fourteen times, so make fourteen copies of the image. Then cut out the pictures with scissors.

◎ The Ritual

On the evening of the new moon, place a mason jar or a cup full of water next to a silver or white tea light or penny candle. Then, read your answers for questions 1 and 2 out loud. Sit with your answers, and when you're ready, light the candle. Next, burn a picture of the mask as you chant or pray for the person/people's facade to also turn to ash. Pray for them to make a critical mistake that will provide the proof you need to bust them.

Place a magnifying glass or the image of a protective deity, spirit guide, animal totem, or ancestor in front of a picture or a symbolic representation of the person/people you want to expose. Leave it in a brightly lit room during the day and a nightlight, flameless candle, or some form of light near the picture after sundown. It should never be allowed to be in the dark! Do this ritual every day and on the night of the full moon after the truth is revealed; thank the moon and whoever or whatever assisted you.

XIX BIG MAMA

If life has been getting you down and you feel your faith wavering, then this ritual is for you.

◎ Prep Work

1. Make a list of all the things you are grateful for in your life.
2. Make a list of all the times in your life when things went wrong and you felt like you're feeling now. Write down how each situation was finally resolved and check for patterns that may give you ideas about what you can do now to resolve the current situation.

3. Create a playlist of uplifting music, sermons, lectures, or meditations. These should provoke optimistic feelings and really energize you.

◎ *The Ritual*

For a minimum of five to twenty minutes every day while you're feeling down, listen to a few selections from your playlist. But don't just listen; really hear whatever the singer, composer, or inspirational speaker is communicating.

Whenever thoughts of hopelessness, failure, or desperation try to take over, take a moment (go to the bathroom if you're at work) and say, "I refuse to submit to defeat; I put my faith in victory; I am victorious" at least four times. You may also use a prayer or chant of your choice. Visualize a beautiful glow forming around you that eventually seeps into every pore and cell of your body. Do this every day until your faith has been restored.

XX
DEM BONES

XX DEM BONES

It you feel that you're in need of a fresh start, then this ritual is for you.

◎ *Prep Work*

1. In your journal, write down the areas of your life that feel stagnant or played out. Are you still happy with your appearance, your wardrobe, your job, your friends, your home, and your usual hangout spots?

2. For every "no" answer, ask yourself if that person or thing is in alignment with the future you desire. If you had your ideal look or wardrobe, won the lottery, got a better education, and so on, would those people or things still be there? Would you still live in your neighborhood? Would you still hang out there? Be honest.

3. Now that you've assessed your situation, what is the judgment? Do you

really like your life or are you just caught in a cycle of tolerating and settling?

4. How is your reputation? Are you happy with it? If not, what would you like it to be? What traits, characteristics, or circumstances prevent you from being perceived as you would like to be perceived? What can you do about it?

◎ *The Ritual*

Before the next new moon, get rid of as many unwanted things as you can afford and unfriend/unfollow people and pages that reflect the old you. Reevaluate everything and everyone in your life from now on as either an asset or a liability to the future you're trying to create.

XXI THE GARDEN

If life is generally good but has become monotonous, then this ritual is for you.

◎ *Prep Work*

1. Make a list of everything you have always wanted to try but never got around to.
2. Make a list of the reasons or excuses why you did not pursue your interests and passions.
3. Do research on how or where you can find these things to try.

◎ *The Ritual*

Once a week for the next four months, try something from your list or simply something new. It could be as small as purchasing a different flavor of bubble gum, exploring a new movie genre, or selecting a place you know nothing about for your next vacation. If you open yourself up to novel experiences, you will learn and grow, which will automatically make life more interesting.

What Happens in the House, Stays in the House

Family Card Reflections and Exercises

The Family cards represent the positive and negative characteristics of ourselves or the people around us. If you're doing a personal reading that has nothing to do with anyone else and you receive a Family card, then it's probably reflecting your energy at that time.

Many people find it difficult to see themselves in certain family cards so they may ignore or gloss over them when they come up. The result of that is a lost opportunity to receive critical insight into the situation about which you're inquiring. This section will help you better understand your personality as it relates to each of the Family cards.

MOTHER of STICKS

MOTHER OF STICKS

When the Mother of Sticks comes up in a reading, reflect on the following:

- Do you have what it takes to lead with strength and conviction?
- Have you lost your swag?
- Are you being overbearing or a bully?
- Make sure you don't look weak in an attempt to look strong.
- Are you aware of the ways you are powerful?

◎ *Exercise*

Ask yourself, In what ways am I most like the Mother of Sticks?

In your journal, list two positive traits and two negative traits.

FATHER of STICKS

FATHER OF STICKS

When the Father of Sticks comes up in a reading, reflect on the following:

- Are you pursuing your constructive passions?
- In what ways can you express your creativity more?
- Are you using your manifestation powers wisely?
- Why do you care so much about that?
- It's time to commit to what inspires you.

◎ *Exercise*

Ask yourself, In what ways am I most like the Father of Sticks?

In your journal, list two positive traits and two negative traits.

DAUGHTER of STICKS

DAUGHTER OF STICKS

When the Daughter of Sticks comes up in a reading, reflect on the following:

- ◌ What does it mean to live with passion?
- ◌ Are you living your life with passion or just "doing what you have to do"?
- ◌ Do you ignore red flags and other signs that something may not be right?
- ◌ Is it time for you to alter your life's course by changing direction?
- ◌ In what areas of your life do you feel stuck?

◎ *Exercise*

Ask yourself, In what ways am I most like the Daughter of Sticks?
In your journal, list two positive traits and two negative traits.

SON of STICKS

SON OF STICKS

When the Son of Sticks comes up in a reading, reflect on the following:

- ◌ How are you expressing your unique talents and gifts?
- ◌ Are you deliberately being contrary, rebellious, or different just to get attention?
- ◌ Are you getting enough exercise?
- ◌ Perhaps that unusual occurrence was the sign you asked for?
- ◌ Temper tantrums don't help the situation.
- ◌ That's great, but are you sure that's the right path for you?
- ◌ Have you been hesitant to explore a new passion or interest?

⊚ *Exercise*

Ask yourself, In what ways am I most like the Son of Sticks?

In your journal, list two positive traits and two negative traits.

MOTHER OF BASKETS

When the Mother of Baskets comes up in a reading, reflect on the following:

- ↺ Are you strong enough to be soft?
- ↺ It's time to be a lover not a fighter.
- ↺ Stop all that whining and fix your face!
- ↺ It's possible to be a nurturing, supportive leader.

⊚ *Exercise*

Ask yourself, In what ways am I most like the Mother of Baskets?

In your journal, list two positive traits and two negative traits.

FATHER OF BASKETS

When the Father of Baskets comes up in a reading, reflect on the following:

- ↺ Just tell them what's really on your mind.
- ↺ Caring is good, clingy isn't.
- ↺ Allow your heart to guide you in this situation.
- ↺ Did you know other people have feelings, too?
- ↺ No one wants to be around someone who is always broody and moody.

◎ *Exercise*

Ask yourself, In what ways am I most like the Father of Baskets?
In your journal, list two positive traits and two negative traits

DAUGHTER OF BASKETS

When the Daughter of Baskets comes up in a reading, reflect on the following:

- ☾ Are you afraid to pursue your dreams?
- ☾ Romance is in the air.
- ☾ Mind your manners.
- ☾ Act your age not your shoe size. Grow up.
- ☾ Are you trying to seduce someone that is clearly not interested?
- ☾ Here's a tissue for those crocodile tears.

◎ *Exercise*

Ask yourself, In what ways am I most like the Daughter of Baskets?
In your journal, list two positive traits and two negative traits.

SON OF BASKETS

When the Son of Baskets comes up in a reading, reflect on the following:

- ☾ A little flirting won't hurt.
- ☾ Didn't your intuition already tell you the answer?
- ☾ Now you know they're really into you—what're you going to do?
- ☾ Are you risking your heart for someone who's emotionally unavailable?

◎ *Exercise*

Ask yourself, In what ways am I most like the Son of Baskets?

In your journal, list two positive traits and two negative traits.

MOTHER of KNIVES

MOTHER OF KNIVES

When the Mother of Knives comes up in a reading, reflect on the following:

- ☊ In what ways are my emotions getting in the way of logic?
- ☊ What is the bottom line?
- ☊ Am I being coldhearted or cruel?
- ☊ Am I making excuses for an abuser?

◎ *Exercise*

Ask yourself, In what ways am I most like the Mother of Knives?

In your journal, list two positive traits and two negative traits.

FATHER of KNIVES

FATHER OF KNIVES

When the Father of Knives comes up in a reading, reflect on the following:

- ☊ It's time to stop walking on eggshells.
- ☊ Will this decision still make sense a few years from now?
- ☊ Consider calling it like you see it.
- ☊ Did you express yourself as clearly and concisely as possible?
- ☊ Is your anger out of control?

○ Do you really dislike that person/those people or do they remind you of what you're not doing, being, or accomplishing?

○ Are you unwittingly exhibiting lack of confidence?

○ Are you speaking your truth?

◎ *Exercise*

Ask yourself, In what ways am I most like the Father of Knives?

In your journal, list two positive traits and two negative traits.

DAUGHTER of KNIVES

DAUGHTER OF KNIVES

When the Daughter of Knives comes up in a reading, reflect on the following:

○ If you're not being heard, what are you going to do about it?

○ Sometimes you must disappoint others to please yourself.

○ What's your point?

○ It's time to seek the truth.

○ Did you have to say it like that?

○ Why are you debating about this?

○ Are you being passive aggressive?

○ Stop stalling and go!

◎ *Exercise*

Ask yourself, In what ways am I most like the Daughter of Knives?

In your journal, list two positive traits and two negative traits.

SON of KNIVES

SON OF KNIVES

When the Son of Knives comes up in a reading, reflect on the following:

- ꍈ Are you prepared to receive an honest answer to your question?
- ꍈ Have you forgone critical analytical thinking in this situation?
- ꍈ This situation may require a new way of thinking, new ideas, or a new approach to succeed.
- ꍈ Stop acting like a brat.
- ꍈ Oaths and promises are sacred.
- ꍈ Are you sure you're not being defensive?
- ꍈ Consider identifying the facts instead of focusing only on your feelings.

◎ *Exercise*

Ask yourself, In what ways am I most like the Son of Knives?
In your journal, list two positive traits and two negative traits.

MOTHER of COINS

MOTHER OF COINS

When the Mother of Coins comes up in a reading, reflect on the following:

- ꍈ Have you considered that what you want might be contrary to what someone you care about needs right now?
- ꍈ Are you the best person to lead right now, or is that your ego talking?
- ꍈ Do you know and understand all the terms and conditions of that investment?
- ꍈ Consistent overspending could cost you sooner than later.

- Helping people out is great, but not every limping dog has to become your pet.
- Are you practical and grounded enough to make it happen? Is your plan down to earth?
- Is that thought, action, or response the most practical or responsible one?
- Have you become so obsessed with saving money that you've become annoying and boring?

◎ Exercise

Ask yourself, In what ways am I most like the Mother of Coins?

In your journal, list two positive traits and two negative traits.

FATHER of COINS

FATHER OF COINS

When the Father of Coins comes up in a reading, reflect on the following:

- What is the commonsense solution to your problem?
- Is that offer in alignment with your values?
- Don't allow overthinking to make you miss out on a potentially great opportunity!
- Treat yourself, but don't overindulge.
- Beware of tacky displays of wealth or privilege.
- Get-rich-quick schemes usually end up achieving the opposite result.
- Just because you can doesn't mean you should.
- Stop ignoring those bill collectors and make a payment arrangement.
- If the situation is not that serious then why are you asking? Let it go.

◎ *Exercise*

Ask yourself, In what ways am I most like the Father of Coins?
In your journal, list two positive traits and two negative traits.

DAUGHTER of COINS

DAUGHTER OF COINS

When the Daughter of Coins comes up in a reading, reflect on the following:

- ↻ Are you as committed as you need to be to do a competent job?
- ↻ If you're about to give up, then you're underestimating how much perseverance is a factor.
- ↻ Are you really too busy or just too lazy?
- ↻ Is the decision you're about to make best for your long-term security?
- ↻ Precisely how many steps will it take to reach your goal?

◎ *Exercise*

Ask yourself, In what ways am I most like the Daughter of Coins?
In your journal, list two positive traits and two negative traits.

SON OF COINS

SON of COINS

When the Son of Coins comes up in a reading, reflect on the following:

- What is the weakest aspect of your plan? Fix it, or come up with a plan B—or even a plan B and C.
- Can you turn this into a new financial opportunity?
- Are you being appreciated for your contribution?
- Is this the right time to make this investment?
- What seeds are you planting by taking this course of action?
- Are your choices in alignment with your ultimate goal?

Exercise

Ask yourself, In what ways am I most like the Son of Coins?

In your journal, list two positive traits and two negative traits.

Working with the Community Cards

Your Role, Responsibilities, and
Manifestations in the World

The Elders cards represent life's larger, more complex themes, while the Community cards represent life as we experience it day to day. When you're clear and resolved about who you are, what you believe, and why you believe it, and you know your purpose, then you're well on your way to achieving genuine contentment.

Fulfillment, however, is another matter entirely, because that has more to do with how you're living and expressing yourself daily. It's great to have arrived at a place of satisfaction with oneself philosophically and spiritually, but if your mundane existence is out of alignment with your truth, then it can be a real bore or make you downright miserable.

This section is about helping you understand the little details about yourself and how you truly feel about your everyday existence. Everyone is a part of several communities simultaneously, and for any community to thrive its members must be aware of their role and responsibilities in it. They must be aware of what their thoughts and actions are manifesting and be conscious of whether their output is constructive or destructive to the whole. Conscious awareness of your true self, issues, and priorities will not only assist you but will ultimately assist the communities that you care about as well.

◎ *Exercise*

Lay each full suit of cards out in a straight line from ace to ten (as seen in the example below). Then, in your journal, answer the following questions for each suit: Sticks, Baskets, Knives, and Coins.

Ace	1	2	3	4	5	6	7	8	9	10

1. Which card reflects what you desire most?
2. How does your desire benefit you, your family, your people, your favorite online community, your country, the land, and so on?
3. How close are you to attaining what you desire to be, do, accomplish, or become?
4. Which card reflects what you hate or fear most?
5. How does that card reflect who you are, who you've been, what you're going through, or what you've been through?

An Interview with Your *Hoodoo Tarot* Deck

If you own more than two tarot decks, you may have realized that each one has its own distinct energy. So much so that some decks seem to be more effective at addressing certain issues than others. It all depends on the energy of the reader and how everyone consciously and subconsciously interacts with the artwork and symbolism of each deck.

After working a long time with a particular deck, it is common for people to develop a special relationship with its unique voice. The interview questions in the following reading will give you more insight into what to look forward to from your *Hoodoo Tarot* deck. To do this reading for yourself, start by shuffling the cards and then pull one card per question.

1	2	3	4	5	6	7

1. What may limit my ability to connect with this deck?
2. What can this deck teach me about myself?
3. What card in this deck will my ancestors use most to speak to me?
4. What is the potential outcome of working with this deck?
5. What do I need to do to become the best reader I can be?
6. What is the greatest benefit of working with this deck?
7. Do you want to be read exclusively for my benefit or for others?

Sample Reading for Arietta

Interpretation

1. **What may limit my ability to connect with this deck?**
   The Six of Knives suggests that Arietta may have a hard time letting *The Hoodoo Tarot* be the tarot deck that it is instead of the ones she is used to. She may be so used to working with other decks that she is unable to go with the flow and is resistant to a change of perspective.

2. **What can this deck teach me about myself?**
   The Grandchildren suggests that Arietta will experience a renewal of faith and a more optimistic perspective on life as a result of working with *The Hoodoo Tarot*.

3. **What card in this deck will my ancestors use most to speak to me?**
   Railroad Bill suggests that Arietta's ancestors will be most active during moments when she lacks confidence and will be there to encourage her to be more assertive and move forward when the time is right.

4. **What is the potential outcome of working with this deck?**
   The Five of Knives suggests that Arietta will be more motivated to resolve conflicts and overcome challenges in her life.

5. **What do I need to do to become the best reader I can be?**
   The Big House suggests that Arietta should work on expecting the unexpected and become more adaptable to change. There may come a time when a reading will provide a shockingly unexpected response, and she will have to be prepared to receive it without falling apart.

6. **What is the greatest benefit of working with this deck?**
The Five of Baskets here suggests that Arietta will have a sense of renewed hope working with *The Hoodoo Tarot*. It will give her the opportunity to work through some of her toughest emotional problems and become a healing force in her life.

7. **Do you want to be read exclusively for my benefit or for others?**
The Two of Knives suggests that Arietta should wait to see how she develops as a reader to determine whether she truly wants the responsibility of reading for other people. It is important for her to be patient and wait until she is certain.

Hoodoo Rooms

It's common all over the world for practitioners of various religious and spiritual ways of life to maintain sacred spaces. The purpose of these spaces is to provide adherents with a safe, often private place to pray, meditate, do divination, study, teach, and/or perform rituals. It is not required for Rootworkers to have an altar or a special room in which to work, but if they have the desire and the space for one, it can be helpful.

Many Rootworkers in the past simply incorporated their sacred objects into their garden and home decor to express the seamless boundary between the sacred and the profane or to be less conspicuous if non-Hoodoo folks were often entertained at the house. Because there were no strict rules about how sacred spaces were supposed to look or be arranged in our tradition, every Rootworker had the opportunity to express themselves as boldly or discreetly as they pleased. No one had the authority to tell another practitioner what colors, textures, patterns, or objects to use, so the possibilities were endless—that is, unless there were taboos passed down from one's elders in the family, a warning was expressed by another trusted practitioner, or if they or someone close to them had a foreboding dream about it; then the Rootworker would make the necessary changes to avoid unnecessary misfortune.

As a middle-class New Yorker who lived with extended family in midtown Manhattan, I didn't have the space to have a Hoodoo room, so I kept a simple altar in the corner of my bedroom as seen on page 114.

Now that I live in the South, I have a front yard, backyard, and a Hoodoo room, so I can get more creative and expand. On page 115

My previous simple altar

is a photo of the much bigger temporary altar I put together a few years ago.

I thoroughly clean the house or shift things around in preparation for the new and full moon, and I change tapestries, altar clothes, and other accents according to the season, so I'm usually quite busy four days before lunar shifts, solstices, and equinoxes. But although the look of my Hoodoo room changes, the permanent presence of ancestor photos, sacred tools, objects, and plants centers my mind on the reality of infinite time and possibilities.

The key to the success of any altar or sacred area is to be crystal clear about what you want to accomplish in that space and how you want to use it. The last thing you want is to arrange and decorate things just right, only to realize later that it isn't functional. First you must decide if your sacred spaces and whatever you do there will be for your eyes only.

My larger altar

Obviously, you will have a lot more freedom to put what you want in there no matter how eccentric or bizarre it may be to outsiders. Do you just want a quiet sanctuary to reflect or a place to dance when the spirit moves you? Really take your time to consider how you want to exist there.

While it's impossible for me to tell you how every Rootworker's sacred space will look, I can share some commonalities among the altars, Hoodoo rooms, or gardens I've seen. I have almost always found the following:

- Statues or figurines
- Strategically placed rocks or stones
- Plants the practitioner uses most in their workings
- A Bible or a favorite quote from the Bible hanging somewhere
- Incense/incense burners

- Representations of beloved animals and/or their actual feathers, teeth, and so on
- Vessels, vases, or mason jars filled with herbs or other materials
- Photos or artwork of beloved ancestors, heroes, magical beings, or even popular icons, celebrities, and advertisements that invoke a particular feeling in the Rootworker or communicate a message to clients and passersby

Figurines and stones in my Hoodoo room

Most importantly, a Hoodoo room, or any other sacred space, regardless of its size, should be clean and well-organized and put you in the mind-set needed to accomplish whatever you're trying to accomplish.

My Hoodoo room,
a close-up view of sacred items

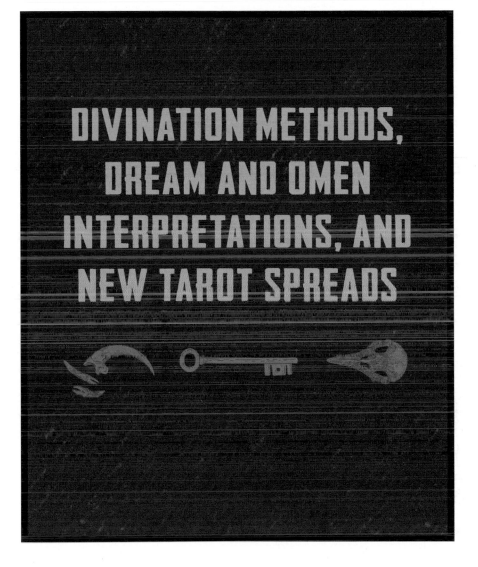

DIVINATION METHODS, DREAM AND OMEN INTERPRETATIONS, AND NEW TAROT SPREADS

Bibliomancy 101

The word *bibliomancy* comes from the Greek *biblio*, meaning "books," and *mancy*, meaning "divination by means of." Obviously, to perform bibliomancy there must be books available, so this form of divination was used by cultures that utilized sacred texts to make important decisions. The referenced texts could be transferred via oral transmission, the written word, or both—for example, the Yoruba Ifa oracle or the Chinese I Ching. However, the written word has remained the most common medium used since ancient times.

In pre-Christian Rome, the works of Homer and Virgil were the most popular texts used to foretell the future. Once Europeans had been fully converted to Christianity with the assistance of Africans who played a significant role in shaping the Nicene and Athanasian Creeds, between the seventh and eighth centuries CE the Bible became the preferred text used throughout Europe. Although the Bible often condemns divination and witchcraft, bibliomancy was still widely used throughout the European Middle Ages.

When Europeans arrived in the sixteenth century, they brought bibliomancy with them. According to the informants of Hoodoo folklorist Harry Middleton Hyatt, Black Americans were familiar with variations throughout the South of the book and key method of receiving prophetic messages from the Bible. The book and key method was still quite common in rural England as late as the nineteenth century. Hyatt's informant 1222 from Brunswick, Georgia, states:

> Well, yo' take a Bible and de 14th chaptah of Exodus, an' yo' take a cord string, but it have to be a large cord string whut will hold de

Bible up, and yo' have two keys. Yo' take de keys an' yo' make a cross wit it. Yo' see, yo' hold one of de key, but chew hol dem both in yore han' lak dis. Aftah yo' read de 14th chaptah of Exodus, yo' put a brown piece of paper in dere—a plain brown piece of paper. . . . An yo' lay it on dat same chaptah, an if yo' wants tuh find out anythin' . . . yo' jes use dis word, "De Holy Bible supposed to be true, an we go tuh fin nuthin but de Word of God, and if dey stole it, de Bible will turn and fall."

The book and key method was used a lot during medieval times to detect heretics and thieves, but there are other techniques for performing bibliomancy. Following is a simple yet effective example:

1. Select a book that deeply resonates with you. It can be a religious text, poetry book, or any genre that is meaningful to you. Any book that you feel changed your life for the better is an optimum choice.
2. Spiritually cleanse the book by purifying it with incense.
3. Meditate for at least five minutes on your question and then, when you're ready, open the book to any page and point your finger to a passage.
4. Take a few moments to contemplate the message you've received and how it's relevant to your situation.
5. In your journal, record the following each time you use the bibliomancy method:
   Book title
   Reason for choosing the book
   Your question
   Incense used
   Selected passage/answer
   Your interpretation

Augury 101

The word *augury* derives from old French and means "interpretation of omens." Augury has been widely practiced all around the world. Depending on the culture, a wise person, magician, priest, or shaman would predict the future based on the behavior of birds or other wild animals. It was their job to determine if said behavior was auspicious or inauspicious, and it was up to either them or another person to do rituals to appease the Gods or spirits if misfortune was predicted.

Every culture has animals they revere more than others, and every culture has animals that they generally despise, are disgusted by, or view with suspicion. Then there are subcultures within a society—such as certain clan kinship groups, members of societies with secrets, and so forth—that have their own perspective on what certain animals signify.

If your ancestors' perspective regarding animal omens has been lost, the creation stories or folktales of your ethnic group and/or clan are potentially good sources of information. Creation stories and folktales in most cultures usually feature animals and identify which ones are considered dangerous, lucky, helpful, associated with the ancestral realm, and so on. Also, see the list on page 123 for some of the animals associated with *The Hoodoo Tarot*.

Another way for aspiring augurs to learn animal symbolism is to learn to carefully observe nature, paying attention to details and listening to your intuition. It would also be helpful to write down your experiences for future reference, making sure to take note of repetitive patterns and the accuracy of your predictions. Don't forget to consult yourself!

◎ *Your Inner Augur*

In your journal, jot down four animals, insects, or birds that you like and four that you dislike.

For each animal, answer the following questions:

1. Why do you like or dislike this animal?
2. What does this animal represent to you?
3. How do you feel when you see this animal?

The following is a list of animals used in *The Hoodoo Tarot* and what they represent.

The Animals of *The Hoodoo Tarot*

Alligator: determination, being "thick skinned," primal instincts, fearlessness

Birds: superior vision, seeing the bigger picture, possibilities, protection from the elements, freedom, caution, purposefulness

Cat: magic, inquisitiveness, gracefulness, protection, darkness, and rebirth

Dog: loyalty, protection, obedience, unconditional love, and friendship

Fish: water, productivity, good luck, and depth of awareness

Florida Black Panther: patience, strength, nobility, superior leadership, and advanced spiritual power

Horses: freedom, mobility, power, and endurance

Kite: divine messages, efficiency, and the ability to see the bigger picture

Owl: ability to see during dark times, seeing different points of view, hidden enemies

Pig: laziness, greed, ignorance, stubbornness, and restlessness

Puma: power, intelligence, quiet self-reflection, and survival skills

Rabbit: speed, agility, caution, fertility, and tricksters

Rooster: protection, alertness, hope, fertility, and bravery

Salamander: resourcefulness, regeneration, balance, vibrancy, and energy

Snail: preparedness, peace, slow progress, and persistence

Snake: transformation, cunning, patience, intuition, adaptability, focus, forward movement, intimidation, lack of emotionality

Turtle: wisdom, retreat, and longevity

Judicial Astrology 101

Judicial astrology is the study of the positions and motions of celestial bodies in the belief that they have an influence over nature and human affairs. This form of astrology was called "judicial" in medieval Europe because it represented God's judgment announced in the stars. By the time the Pilgrims arrived in North America in the seventeenth century, astrology had already begun to fade as a serious scientific approach in Europe. However, astrology remained popular among all classes of society.

Astrological almanacs provided colonists with the information they craved regarding the influence of the stars on nature and their personal lives. In fact, as pastime reading material, they were as popular as the Bible. The first almanac by Nathaniel Ames had a circulation of sixty thousand copies in 1671. Benjamin Banneker, a free Black man, published his wildly successful almanac in 1795, which was distributed in Pennsylvania, Delaware, Maryland, and Virginia. So, despite the proclamations by the misinformed that America's obsession with New Age subjects like astrology is a contemporary phenomenon, it is more accurate to say that interest in astrology is part of the genetic fabric of our society.

The biblical references to astrology no doubt increased the faith in its usefulness, as it would be hard to ignore the following passages:

The heavens declare the glory of God;
the skies proclaim the work of his hands.
Day after day they pour forth speech;
night after night they reveal knowledge.

PSALM 19:1–2

After Jesus was born in Bethlehem in Judea, during the time
of King Herod, Magi from the east came to Jerusalem and
asked, "Where is the one who has been born king of the
Jews? We saw his star when it rose and have come
to worship him. . . ."
Then Herod called the Magi secretly and found out from
them the exact time the star had appeared. He sent them to
Bethlehem and said, "Go and search carefully for the child.
As soon as you find him, report to me, so that I too may go
and worship him."

MATTHEW 2:1–8

In every matter of wisdom and understanding about which
the king questioned them, he found them [astrologers] ten
times better than all the magicians and enchanters in his
whole kingdom.

DANIEL 1:20

There will be signs in the sun, moon and stars. On the earth,
nations will be in anguish and perplexity at the roaring and
tossing of the sea.

LUKE 21:25

He is the Maker of the Bear and Orion, the Pleiades and the
constellations of the South.

JOB 9:9

There is no mention of astrology being one of the condemned eso-teric sciences in the Old Testament. Instead, the repulsion of astrology can be traced back to the personal opinion of Augustine of Hippo, the Berber philosopher and theologian from Numidia who hated astrology and whose writings were key to the development of Western philosophy.

Cleromancy 101

Cleromancy is the casting of lots in the form of bones, sticks, shells, and so on. It is a divination method that has been practiced in America, Africa, Europe, and Asia since ancient times. Rune (Norse), merindinlogun (Yoruban), Mo (Tibetan), and tzite (Mayan) divination are a few examples.

Cleromancy was also an acceptable practice to the biblical fathers and the disciples of Jesus. In fact, the casting of lots is mentioned over seventy times in the Bible. Following are some examples:

The lot is cast into the lap, but its every decision is from the Lord.

PROVERBS 16:33

Then they prayed, "Lord, you know everyone's heart. Show us which of these two you have chosen to take over this apostolic ministry, which Judas left to go where he belongs." Then they cast lots, and the lot fell to Matthias; so he was added to the eleven apostles.

ACTS 1:24–26

When they had crucified him, they divided up his clothes by casting lots.

MATTHEW 27:35

They divided them impartially by casting lots, for there were officials of the sanctuary and officials of God among the descendants of both Eleazar and Ithamar.

1 Chronicles 24:5

Then the sailors said to each other, "Come, let us cast lots to find out who is responsible for this calamity." They cast lots and the lot fell on Jonah.

Jonah 1:7

Casting the lot settles disputes and keeps strong opponents apart.

Proverbs 18:18

Joshua then cast lots for them in Shiloh in the presence of the LORD, and there he distributed the land to the Israelites according to their tribal divisions.

Joshua 18:10

We—the priests, the Levites and the people—have cast lots to determine when each of our families is to bring to the house of our God at set times each year a contribution of wood to burn on the altar of the LORD our God, as it is written in the Law.

Nehemiah 10:34

They also cast lots, just as their relatives the descendants of Aaron did, in the presence of King David and of Zadok, Ahimelech, and the heads of families of the priests and of the Levites. The families of the oldest brother were treated the same as those of the youngest.

1 Chronicles 24:31

The leaders of the people settled in Jerusalem. The rest of the people cast lots to bring one out of every ten of them to live in Jerusalem, the holy city, while the remaining nine were to stay in their own towns.

NEHEMIAH 11:1

After you have written descriptions of the seven parts of the land, bring them here to me and I will cast lots for you in the presence of the LORD our God.

JOSHUA 18:6

Young and old alike, teacher as well as student, cast lots for their duties.

1 CHRONICLES 25:8

Be sure that the land is distributed by lot. What each group inherits will be according to the names for its ancestral tribe.

NUMBERS 26:55

He was chosen by lot, according to the custom of the priesthood, to go into the temple of the Lord and burn incense.

LUKE 1:9

Then Saul prayed to the LORD, the God of Israel, "Why have you not answered your servant today? If the fault is in me or my son Jonathan, respond with Urim, but if the men of Israel are at fault, respond with Thummim." Jonathan and Saul were taken by lot, and the men were cleared. Saul said, "Cast the lot between me and Jonathan my son." And Jonathan was taken.

1 SAMUEL 14:41–42

*For Haman son of Hammedatha, the Agagite, the enemy
of all the Jews, had plotted against the Jews to destroy them
and had cast the pur (that is, the lot) for their ruin and
destruction.*

ESTHER 9:24

———◆◇▶———

The resurgence of interest in Conjure has reignited interest in American cleromancy, which consisted of animal bones, crystals, rocks, beads, and other small objects chosen by practitioners. This method of reading was used by the Cherokee and others throughout the Southeast. Every family, tribe, or individual diviner had their own way of selecting, collecting, and cleansing objects, using prayers and invocations, deciding how many objects to use and how to cast, interpreting symbolism, and/or performing rituals. A person may choose to learn bone reading from a respected diviner and inherit their methodology that way.

Cartomancy 102

In my first book, *Rootwork: Using the Folk Magick of Black America for Love, Money, and Success,* I gave a list of basic meanings for each card and the "proper" etiquette for playing-card divination (i.e., "Cartomancy 101"). Here, I will again share the meanings of the playing cards as well as how I read them and conceptualize them while doing so ("Cartomancy 102").

No one knows for sure where playing cards originated, but most scholars agree that they originated somewhere in the East and traveled to the West. What we do know for certain is that playing-card imagery and symbolism changed to reflect the culture of the people who adopted it. While playing cards were primarily used as a tool of amusement for most people who owned them, regardless of their geographic location, there were divinatory meanings ascribed to them as well. The occult interpretation of the cards would, therefore, be as diverse as the ever-changing aesthetic depending on the religious, spiritual, and philosophical viewpoints of the diviner. So there is nothing to stop anyone, anywhere, at any time from changing the colors and the symbols, the appearance of the face cards, the occupation/social status of the characters, or the divinatory meanings.

FOUR-CARD SPREAD

I typically use a four-card spread when I am doing readings with playing cards. When doing a reading for yourself or someone else, first shuffle the cards, then pull one card for each of the four spread positions below and place it in front of you as shown.

131

1. Your/their problem or concern
2. Your/their primary inner conversation about the problem/concern
3. Your/their secret weapon
4. The best solution—what should be avoided or what new belief/ attitude is needed for you/them to be victorious

THE CARDS AND THEIR MEANINGS

The following sections describe the meanings of the jokers, face cards, and aces.

Big Joker

The Big Joker is the trickster. Tricksters are usually human or animal characters in stories designed to teach moral lessons with humor. Tricksters may be heroes or villains, trustworthy or untrustworthy, mean or funny, helpful or harmful. They're usually smart and appear when the main character is on a journey and cause much chaos or confusion along the way. Trickster tales may be found all around the world, but Black American/American Indian trickster tales don't emphasize the necessity that moral violations be punished as is common in European or Euro-American folktales. Instead, the focus is on how the trickster can outsmart a formidable opponent or a challenging situation to get what they want. Jerry the mouse from the *Tom and Jerry* cartoon series and Bugs Bunny and are excellent examples of the American trickster style.

Likewise, when this card comes up, it can be an indicator that the querent or someone else related to the reading are exhibiting the characteristics of the trickster. And if the trickster appears in placement one or two of the four-card spread, there is an especially good chance that someone may deliberately be trying to be slick, manipulative, and/or deceptive. The appearance of the trickster in placements three or four may suggest that the querent use more cunning or strategy to get the results they're seeking or that they seriously reflect on their situation and seek the moral of the story so they may learn from it.

Little Joker

The Little Joker represents the querent's rationalizations or excuses for doing things they know deep down inside they shouldn't be doing or aren't in their best interests. When this card comes up in the second or third placement, the querent or someone else involved in the situation is probably guilty of exactly that.

Queens

The Queens are the principal authorities. In keeping with the matrilineal nature of traditional southern Black American/American Indian culture, the Queens are the foundation of power and authority of each "family," or suit. She may represent individuals or one's maternal-line ancestors if she appears in placement four.

Kings

The Kings provide nourishment and protection for the Queens. The King is equal to the Queen, but his role is to ensure that the Queen's basic needs are met, and she is protected. When a King appears in placement one or two, the querent should consider how they may be prioritizing wants over needs in a situation. They should also consider if they or someone else are violating boundaries and what should be done to correct the security breach. The King may represent specific individuals if he appears in placements one, two, or three or a direct message from one's paternal-line ancestors if he appears in placement four.

Jacks

The Jacks serve the Queen of their suit. The role of the Jack is to remind the querent to consider how their energy could be of best use in a situation. Good servants are obedient, efficient, productive, pleasant, flexible, reliable, and honest. Everyone at some point must be of service to something or someone else. When a Jack appears in any placement, it may be because the querent or someone else is unwilling to do what needs to be done for the good of the whole. If a Jack appears in placement four, then failure to properly serve may signal the arrival of feelings of shame, financial difficulties, arguments, or other misfortunes in the querent's family.

Aces

The Aces represent the essence of their suit (see the Ace Elements at Work section for more information).

THE SUITS AND THEIR ELEMENTS

The suits represent the four elements—Air, Earth, Fire, and Water. Each suit/element has characteristics that make it unique and distinguishable from the others, and each face card and Ace in a suit has a particular association with the element as shown in the lists below.

Spades—Air

Positive characteristics: visionary, open-minded, intelligent, future oriented, truth seeking, memorious

Negative characteristics: easily bored, hyperanalytical, scatterbrained, superficial/lacking depth

Air associations: queen—wind; king—breezes; jack—breath; Ace—one's internal conversation/inner narrative

Diamonds—Earth

Positive characteristics: stable, reliable, persevering, cautious, calm, well organized

Negative characteristics: judgmental, pessimistic, rigid, myopic, boring

Earth associations: Queen—Mother Earth; King—minerals, Jack—fungi; Ace—what a person values most

Clubs—Fire

Positive characteristics: quick thinking, creative, inspiring, ambitious, goal oriented, transformative

Negative characteristics: hotheaded, hasty, domineering, prideful, careless

Fire associations: Queen—lightning; King—bushfires; Jack—the fire of human desire; Ace—the fire of passion

Hearts—Water

Positive characteristics: imaginative, intuitive, nurturing, empathetic, flexible, compassionate, spiritual

Negative characteristics: moody, querulous, hypersensitive, illogical, unfocused

Water associations: Queen—sea; King—rivers; Jack—tributaries (creeks, streams, etc.); Ace—source of the querent's faith

ACE ELEMENTS AT WORK

Here are some examples to give you an idea of how the suits' elements work with specific cards—in this case the Aces. When an Ace appears in placement one or two of a four-card spread, it may indicate that the querent or someone else is exhibiting the negative qualities of that Ace's element. When an Ace appears in placement three, it means that success is more likely by exhibiting more of that element's positive qualities. If the Ace is in the fourth position, it may indicate that the situation may be neutralized or improved by making an ancestral offering symbolized by one or more of the Ace's elements as follows:

Air: saying prayers, burning incense, singing or playing their favorite music

Earth: laying out food, minerals, metals, art, money, flowers, herbs, or plants, moving the body or dancing

Fire: lighting candles, a bonfire, or a campfire in their honor

Water: bathing in or washing spiritual tools with water from sources sacred to your ancestors, offering beverages enjoyed or considered sacred by your ancestors

SAMPLE READINGS

Here are two playing-card sample readings using my four-card spread. Note that I've repeated the significance of the card placements here for convenience.

1. Your/their problem or concern
2. Your/their primary inner conversation about the problem/concern
3. Your/their secret weapon
4. The best solution—what should be avoided or what new belief/attitude is needed for you/them to be victorious

Sample Reading 1

Querent: What can I do to be a better girlfriend?

Interpretation

1. The Two of Clubs suggests that the querent may be taking her relationship for granted by being lazy and/or inattentive to her partner.

2. The Nine of Hearts indicates that the querent naively believes that things will just magically work out because they love each other. She has told herself that she doesn't need to do her absolute best anymore because they're going to be together no matter what she does or doesn't do. Big mistake.

3. The Queen of Diamonds implies that she may have learned from her mother, a mother figure, or a woman she admires that true love is simply being present. The querent is aware that her behavior may be off, but her belief that minimal effort is okay is very strong. In this case, her secret weapon is the part of her that knows she needs to step up her game. The querent must allow this voice complete expression by being honest about what she is doing wrong or needs to work on to be a better girlfriend.

4. The Jack of Spades in this context indicates that the querent's partner has mentioned their dissatisfaction but may not be the type to repeat themselves. Instead, they keep their feelings to themselves and suffer in silence to keep the peace. The querent may believe that things are better than they are because of this, which may lead to a shocking and "sudden" breakup in the future. If the querent genuinely wants to be a better girlfriend, she will recognize that her partner's concerns should be addressed via a solution-based discussion as soon as possible.

Sample Reading 2
Querent: Should I start my own business?

Interpretation

1. The Five of Spades indicates that the querent has suffered a devastating loss that led him to the conclusion that he should start his own business. He revealed that he was fired from his job a few months ago, and it has been a huge emotional and financial strain.

2. The Two of Diamonds suggests that the querent believes that starting his own business will bring about positive changes in his life after a long period of suffering.

3. The Four of Hearts indicates that the querent needs to work on letting go of the disappointment and bitterness of losing his job. Now would not be the most auspicious time to begin a new venture. He would be wise to get help or do some soul searching until he's ready, willing, and able to stop crying over spilled milk and move on.

4. The Seven of Spades implies that the querent might have a shot at success if he meticulously plans next steps and avoids taking shortcuts and unnecessary risks.

This four-card spread is a helpful tool to use whenever you or someone you know needs it. You can keep a record of each of your readings in your journal using the outline below:

Four-Card Spread for [name]
Your/their question:
1. Your/their problem or concern:
2. Your/their primary inner conversation about the problem/concern:
3. Your/their secret weapon:
4. The best solution: What should be avoided or what new belief/attitude is needed for me/them to be victorious?
Your interpretation:

Dreams and Omens

Neutralizing Negativity and Accentuating Positivity Using The Hoodoo Tarot

In *The Hoodoo Tarot* book, I explained how important augury (the interpretation of omens) and oneiromancy (the interpretation of dreams) were to Rootworkers for the purpose of neutralizing negativity or accentuating positivity.

For example, if you or someone else dreamed that the lucky horseshoe above your front door fell and broke, then that would be a good time to do a reading to find out what's going on. If your reading appears to confirm impending misfortune, sadness, or hard times, then it is time to act to neutralize the negativity.

◎ *Neutralizing Negativity*
Here's a seven-step process for neutralizing negativity:

1. Assess yourself. Have you been feeling "off" or receiving other foreboding signs or messages lately? What were they or how long have you been feeling that way?

2. Assess the source. If you or whoever saw an ominous sign or disturbing message, consider how accurate your/their visions have been in the past at predicting misfortune. If your/their track record has been on point, then there is no reason to doubt the validity of the omen or dream.

3. Do a reading for clarification. If the omen or dream is still too abstract and you're still unsure, then do a two-card reading for clarification.

For example:

Card 1: What is the nature of the misfortune/challenge being communicated?

Card 2: What can I do to prevent this from happening or soften the blow?

4. Remain calm. If you received disappointing results, please try to remain calm. It happens. Take your time to feel whatever emotions come up, and don't resume this exercise until you have gotten a grip. Otherwise you will be functioning from hysteria, which limits your reasoning faculty and your ability to hear your inner voice, ancestors, God/gods, or guides.

5. Be holistic. Consider all the advice associated with card 2 in relation to your problem. In other words, brainstorm what you can do on a basic, practical level to help you get through this. Sometimes spiritual people tend to jump right to ritual work to solve their problems—principally, to avoid facing character flaws or poor choices that led to the current situation. For example, if the omen/dream predicts a breakup and you receive the Courting card as a solution, don't just dash to the kitchen to make a honey jar or to your local sex shop to spice things up! It may be time for you and your significant other to have an honest conversation and evaluate if the relationship is still worth all the glaze and seasoning in the first place.

6. Do your best and forget the rest. Once you've covered all your bases on every realm and on every level, then there is nothing left to do but wait. Worrying never fixes anything. Remember, people always operate based on faith regardless of their religious, philosophical, or spiritual path. It is up to each of us whether we will choose to have faith in the worst possible outcome or the best possible outcome. The future and all the possibilities contained within it are not here yet, so neither position can be absolutely proved or disproved. However, there is no question about which attitude will have you anxious, furious, depressed, sick, crying, fretting, whining, or losing sleep. Think about it.

7. Affirm the outcome. If you've decided that you're going to successfully get through whatever life throws your way, congratulations! Now it's time to place card two someplace you can see it and take time every day to affirm the best possible outcome.

◎ *Accentuating Positivity*

So, if you've been feeling a big positive change coming (it's vague, but you know it's on the way), your palms have been itching a lot lately (money is coming), or your cousin dreamed of fish after you mentioned you're trying to conceive (you are or will be pregnant soon), great!

If you don't want to spoil the surprise by doing a reading, then don't! If you want to remain focused on what you want to materialize, though, then here is one simple option:

○ Look through the deck and pick four cards that represent what you would like to be, see, do, or experience when the money, the baby, the promotion, or whatever the omen/dream is predicting finally happens in 3-D.

○ Put the four cards on your altar, take a picture to use as your screensaver, or place them somewhere else to remind you of what you want to manifest.

If you would like to confirm what you or someone else has been feeling, seeing, or dreaming, then repeat steps 1–7 above but change the focus/language to reflect the desirability of the outcomes predicted. For example, the two-card reading suggested in step 3 would be worded as follows:

Card 1: What is the nature of the fortune/joyous occurrence being communicated?

Card 2: What can I do to ensure the most auspicious outcome possible?

If you feel you need more information about a dream or nightmare before you can neutralize negativity or accentuate positivity, writing the following prompts in your journal and recording the results of your nightmare or dream analysis might be helpful:

Analysis of the nightmare I had on [date]:

Description of the nightmare:

How did it make me feel?

Card 1: What is the nature of the misfortune/challenge being communicated?

Card pulled:

My interpretation:

Card 2: What can I do to prevent this from happening or soften the blow?

Card pulled:

My interpretation:

Analysis of the dream I had on [date]:

Description of the dream:

How did it make me feel?

Card 1: What is the nature of the fortune/joyous occurrence being communicated?

Card pulled:

My interpretation:

Card 2: What can I do to ensure the most auspicious outcome possible?

Card pulled:

My interpretation:

Good- and Bad-Luck Omens and Behaviors

The Hoodoo Tarot book included a lot of information regarding lucky and unlucky omens and behaviors and their remedies. The following is a list of others I heard growing up or from other Hoodoo folks. If there is no remedy listed, it doesn't mean there isn't one, it just means I haven't come across one yet.

- If you stub your right foot on the way to conducting business, that's good luck. If you stub your left foot on the way to conducting business, that's bad luck.
  Remedy: If you stubbed your left foot, then go back the way you came. Say a quick prayer and start over to reset the situation.
- If a bird flies into the house, it's a sign of death.
  Remedy: Sweep in front of your house and wash the front and back doors. Keep your front porch and back porch light on for seven nights.
- If you break a mirror, that is seven years of bad luck.
  Remedy: Feed seven children, old people, or fools at no charge to them as soon as possible.
- If a child cries incessantly for three days for no discernible reason, someone close to you will die.
  Remedy: See remedy for the second bullet item.
- If your ear is ringing or your eye twitches, someone is talking badly about you to someone else.
  Remedy: Recite Matthew 7:1–2 and spit on the ground.

- If your foot gets swept with a broom, it's very bad luck.
  Remedy: Immediately spit on the broom or throw salt on it.
- If you or someone else puts your purse (or whatever you carry your money in) on the floor, you will be broke.
  Remedy: Remove it from the floor immediately and place it on something to elevate it.
- Never allow children to walk behind you when you're in public. Always make sure they are beside or in front of you at all times.
- Don't place cash near lighters or matches, or it will make you lose money.
- If you're pregnant don't visit the zoo or your child may be ugly.
  Remedy: If you must visit the zoo, cover your belly button with a Band-Aid or a sash underneath your shirt.
- Pay for items with your right hand and receive the merchandise with your left hand so your money comes back to you quicker.
- Pray over seeds before planting.
- It's bad luck to kiss a baby on the lips. It will make them sick or fussy.
- Bathe in living water, a.k.a. flowing water (rivers, creeks, or waterfalls), during the new moon to purify and rejuvenate yourself spiritually.
- If you have to cut the fingernails of a child under one year old, discard the clippings on sacred ground (for example, a church). Otherwise, the child may grow up to be dishonest or a thief.
- Don't sweep in a bedroom where a sleeping baby is present; it will bring the child misfortune.
- Don't eat heavy or sugary foods after sundown. It will make receiving spiritual messages while you sleep much easier.
- Sweep from the back of the house to the front of the house to more effectively remove unlucky or stagnant energy.
- Bless your plants by giving them water you have prayed over.
- Fast and pray for four days, eating only bread and water, during challenging times. You will be blessed with clarity and/or a solution to your problems.

- Placing hats on the bed is bad luck.
  Remedy: Remove the hat immediately and hang it up properly.
- If you're walking with someone, don't allow objects to come between you.
  Remedy: Say, "Bread and butter."
- Don't whistle in the house (especially at night), or you'll attract malevolent spirits.
- Don't put your shoes on the wrong feet, or you'll be led down the wrong path.
- It's extremely bad luck to eat food or drink water where a tragedy took place.
- Never take your old broom to your new home, or you will bring your old problems with you.
  Remedy: Break your old broom in half and throw it away the day you move out.
- Don't wash clothes or sweep on New Year's Day, or you will wash or sweep away your blessings.
- On New Year's Day, eat collard greens, cornbread, and black-eyed peas to ensure a prosperous new year.
- It's very bad luck for a woman to be the first person to walk across your threshold on New Year's Day.
  Remedy: If you live with a man, then ask him to walk out of the house and back in. If you don't, then ask a male neighbor or a friend to cross your threshold.
- Hang a horseshoe above your front door with the ends pointing upward to attract good fortune.
- To prevent or remove negativity from your home, burn cedar leaves.
- Place small mirrors facing outward in every window of your home to protect yourself and your family from the negative thoughts of enemies.
- Don't dispose of your hair in the garbage; burn it, flush it, or place it in flowing water.

- To protect infants, place a piece of their hair in the Bible.
- To protect your home from malevolent forces or magic, place an owl feather above the front door of your home.
- Face the shoes of everyone you live with in the same direction to maintain harmony.
- Place two alligator statues on your porch to protect your home, one facing east and the other facing west.
- Scatter coins in and around your home to attract more money.
- Place brick dust in front of all the entrances to your home. If someone is secretly your enemy and they enter, then their true feelings and intentions will be exposed.
- Don't place scissors or knives on the bed, or they'll cut your luck or money in half.
- It's bad luck to cut a child's hair before their first birthday.
- Never let a pregnant woman cut or style your hair, or it will start to break or fall out.
- To reveal hidden enemies in a dream, place an owl feather underneath your pillow or mattress.
- Wear a silver coin around your ankle for spiritual protection.

New Tarot Spreads

This chapter explores eleven new tarot spreads to answer a variety of questions that you might be facing.

In each case, shuffle the cards, ask your first question, pull one card, and set it in front of you. Then ask the second question, pull another card, and set that card in front of you to the right of the first card. Do not reshuffle between questions. Continue the process, placing each new card to the right of the previous one, until you have asked all of your questions. Note that each card position, numbered left to right starting at one, relates to the numbered statements given for each spread.

If you need more detail about a particular statement than the original card provides, draw an additional "clarifying" card. Pulling a clarifying card is an intuitive decision that the reader makes. The clarifying card is usually placed below the original card.

SUNDOWN SPREAD

```
┌─────────┐
│         │
│    1    │
│         │
└─────────┘
```

It is a common practice for many readers to pull a single card in the morning before starting their day. This practice is known as the Card of the Day Spread. It is typically done as a focal point for meditation in preparation to meet the day's challenges.

The Sundown Spread builds on this notion, but it is meant to give you an idea of how well you managed the day's challenges. It can be a very useful exercise for self-reflection as you wind down right before bedtime. Pull one card before bedtime and consider how the card's meaning relates to how you responded to any difficulties during the day.

Sample Reading

Shanice was told by her supervisor at the fast-food restaurant that she has been underperforming lately and that if she didn't improve soon, she would be let go. Shanice felt attacked and quit on the spot. On her way home she racked her brain trying to figure out how she was going to pay the rent next month. Later that evening she pulled one card for a Sundown Spread and received the Eight of Sticks.

Interpretation

Shanice needed to seriously get a grip! Her hyperemotional, impulsive action had left her in dire straits. If she disagreed with her supervisor's assessment of her performance, she should have utilized speed by immediately beginning her new job search. That's considerably less stressful than dreading an eviction notice.

NEW MOON SPREAD

The New Moon Spread can help you let go of the old and bring in the new. Pull one card as you ask each of the following questions, laying the cards out in a row from left to right.

1. What do I need to shed from the last lunar cycle?
2. What intentions should I set to grow this lunar cycle?
3. What attitude should I cultivate to bring my goals and intentions to fruition?

Sample Reading

Quetzalli has been feeling stuck lately. Generally, things are the same in her life, but there is something nagging her that she can't quite put her finger on.

Interpretation

1. **What do I need to shed from the last lunar cycle?**
   The Ten of Sticks suggests Quetzalli may be overburdened but has been ignoring her needs so long she doesn't realize that eventually even pack mules have a limit. It's time for her to identify her top current priorities and only focus on those. Then she needs to vow to delegate tasks to others when possible and refuse to take on any additional obligations until she's properly and thoroughly rejuvenated.
2. **What intentions should I set to grow this lunar cycle?**
   The Seven of Sticks implies that Quetzalli may have people around her who may feel entitled to every last drop of her energy. She has

put up with being treated like a juice box so long that they may become combative or resentful when she informs them that she is going to be looking out for herself a lot more than she has in the past. If Quetzalli has any hope of having any peace or more time to focus on what energizes her, she will become prepared to establish and enforce her boundaries.

3. **What attitude should I cultivate to bring my goals and intentions to fruition?**

Aunt Caroline indicates that Quetzalli should embrace the fact that things will change now. Her insistence on protecting her energy may strengthen some relationships or shift or dissolve them completely. She may even begin to see herself and others differently because of the entire experience. Quetzalli will feel better by going with the flow.

FULL MOON SPREAD

The Full Moon Spread can help you recognize your accomplishments, take accountability for your mistakes, and provide advice for how to best move froward for the remainder of the month until the next new moon.

1. What have I manifested since the new moon?
2. What is the full moon illuminating for me now?
3. What do my ancestors wish me to know?

Sample Reading

Jenna's ex, who broke her heart, contacted her even though she made it expressly clear that she wanted no contact. Now she is perplexed and annoyed by the audacity of the attempt to communicate.

Interpretation

1. **What have I manifested since the new moon?**

   The Ace of Knives suggests that she may have manifested an opportunity to get the clarity she sought but never received concerning the breakup. Even if she has since moved on, perhaps there is one critical detail that if known, would shift her perception on the entire situation.

2. **What is the full moon illuminating for me now?**

   The Seven of Coins indicates that the full moon is trying to shine light on the seeds she has sown and the choices she has made in the past.

3. **What do my ancestors wish me to know?**

   Gullah Jack implies that Jenna should take time to reflect and that it's okay to change her mind. People often fear taking a different stance on an issue because they feel vulnerable uprooting.

BIRTHDAY SPREAD

I started doing a Birthday Spread the evening before my birthday to reflect on my accomplishments, disappointments, and to brainstorm solutions. I've done this for more than ten years, and I always awaken on my birthday feeling refreshed, clear, and ready to face my next turn around the sun.

1. What do I need to leave behind from the past year?
2. What is the theme of the year ahead?
3. What should I do more of to enrich my life and be happier?

```
┌─────┐┌─────┐┌─────┐
│     ││     ││     │
│  1  ││  2  ││  3  │
│     ││     ││     │
└─────┘└─────┘└─────┘
```

Sample Reading

Bryan just celebrated his twenty-ninth birthday and wants to know what's in store for the year ahead.

Interpretation

1. **What do I need to leave behind from the past year?**

   The Ace of Sticks indicates that Bryan may have been distracted and gotten in his own way a lot. As a result, he may have missed key opportunities to significantly improve his life.

2. **What is the theme of the year ahead?**

   The Eight of Coins suggests that the central theme of Bryan's twenty-ninth year is personal and professional development. It may be time to learn new skills, advance the skills he already has, enroll in school, and/or rededicate himself to the achievement of his long-term goals.

3. **What should I do more of to enrich my life and be happier?**

   The Nine of Knives implies that Bryan may have gotten off track because he was anxious or depressed. His mental state was not healthy, so he probably made many unhealthy choices, which only made things worse. Bryan would probably benefit from seeking professional help to better understand how he got to where he is and how to heal. Bryan would be much happier if he got the nurturing and support he so desperately needs.

RITUAL WRAP-UP SPREAD

Once the ritual is over, you may find it helpful to ask a few follow-up questions to determine what additional things may be done to further increase your chance of success.

1. What have I manifested during the ritual that will soon come into my conscious awareness?
2. What practical, tangible next steps do I need to take now to realize my goal?
3. What feedback are my ancestors giving me regarding the success of the ritual?

Sample Reading

Miriam just completed an online prosperity ritual with her sister circle. She's energized and excited and wants to know if her efforts will bear fruit and how.

Interpretation

1. **What have I manifested during the ritual that will soon come into my conscious awareness?**

   The Seven of Knives suggests she may not know one or several of the women in her sister circle as well as she thought she did. One of her "sisters" might be deceptive or secretly doesn't want the best for Miriam. She may have expected the prosperity ritual to bring her cash or baubles, but what it will reveal is the deceiver's true colors.

2. **What practical, tangible next steps do I need to make now to realize my goal?**

Dr. Grant indicates that now is the time for Miriam to quietly tend to her own affairs and patiently wait for the truth to reveal itself. This is not the time to post about secret enemies or imply that there is a problem at all. It's time to be still, be cool, listen, and observe.

3. **What feedback are my ancestors giving me regarding the success of the ritual?**

The Nine of Baskets implies that the ritual was a huge success! Miriam may feel disappointed that one of her girls was exposed as a phony, but the ancestors are reminding her that knowledge is wealth.

THE BIG HOUSE HEALING TRAUMA SPREAD

When something happens in our lives that leaves us feeling devastated or depressed, it can be difficult to identify our feelings beyond the pain. This spread will aid in you in that process.

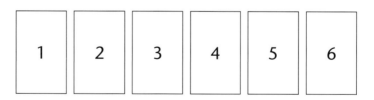

1. How did this traumatic event affect my life the most?
2. How did this traumatic event affect my relationships with others?
3. What actions do I need to take to heal?
4. How can I use the lessons from this experience to grow emotionally and spiritually?

5. What is blocking my ability to successfully transmute the negative to positive?

6. What are clear, tangible signs of change in my life that will prove my healing journey is successful?

Sample Reading

Evelyn grew up watching her stepfather physically and emotionally abuse her mother. She is tired of being haunted by the memories of those horrible times and desperately wants to move on.

Interpretation

1. **How did this traumatic event affect my life the most?**
   The Eight of Baskets suggests that Evelyn may have difficulty maintaining or committing to relationships because deep down inside she doesn't trust people.

2. **How did this traumatic event affect my relationships with others?**
   The Five of Coins implies that Evelyn may have made a lot of people who trusted her feel sad and worthless.

3. **What actions do I need to take to heal?**
   The Seven of Baskets indicates that Evelyn needs to get her head out of the clouds to resolve her issues. This card indicates she has no idea how deeply she has been affected and how much pain she causes because of what she witnessed as a child.

4. **How can I use the lessons from this experience to grow emotionally and spiritually?**
   The Daughter of Knives suggests that Evelyn will grow on every level if she learns the value of solution-based thinking and taking

action when something is wrong. She watched her mother endure unceasing torture and her failure to be proactive about eliminating the problem. Now Evelyn is doing it, too.

5. **What is blocking my ability to successfully transmute the negative to positive?**
   The Nine of Sticks indicates that Evelyn may say she wants to be free but doesn't really believe that it can happen.

6. **What are clear, tangible signs of change in my life that will prove my healing journey is successful?**
   The Ten of Knives implies that Evelyn will continue to be discerning about who to trust, but she will no longer fear emotional intimacy with others as she did before. This will not happen overnight, but Evelyn is determined not to allow the past to ruin her future.

DIFFICULT ANCESTRY SPREAD

We are all affected by the choices past generations have made. Sometimes our families still suffer from an ancestor's cruelty, selfishness, addictions, or weaknesses even if we never met them. This spread will help you determine the best way to move forward.

1. What was the fundamental rationale for the behavior of my troubled ancestor(s) as they understood it?
2. How have the actions of my troubled ancestor(s) affected the family the most?
3. What is the healthiest attitude to have toward my troubled ancestor(s)?
4. As the embodiment of this ancestor(s) in this space, place, and time,

how may I atone for their wrongdoing and restore honor and balance to our family?

5. How should this atonement work look and feel?

6. What will I begin to see, feel, or experience once the healing begins?

Sample Reading

David discovered in his late father's journal that his dad was a victim of sexual abuse by his grandmother from the age of two until he was nine years old. David was shocked, disgusted, and angry. He was close to his late grandmother, and he could never imagine her capable of doing such a thing! The relationship David had with his grandma was wholesome and perfect. So he convinced himself that his father was delusional or that there must be some other explanation—that is, until he showed his older sister the journal, and she confirmed that she heard a rumor that their grandmother and her uncle had molested other children in the family. David practices ancestor veneration and doesn't know how to process what he's learned or what he should do about it.

Interpretation

1. **What was the fundamental rationale for the behavior of my troubled ancestor(s) as they understood it?**

   The Ten of Coins suggests there may be a long legacy of abuse in David's family that he didn't know about. David's grandmother just continued this shameful, destructive legacy without much thought about the consequences. There was an unspoken agreement among the family's members not to discuss this toxic legacy so everyone could pretend that nothing happened.

2. **How have the actions of my troubled ancestor(s) affected the family the most?**

   The Mother of Baskets implies that many family members are emotionally unstable, people pleasers, or pushovers.

3. **What is the healthiest attitude to have toward my troubled ancestor(s)?**

   The Three of Sticks indicates that David should keep the big picture in mind. The issue is much deeper than just his grandmother and great-granduncle. This had been an issue in the family before both were born. Instead of allowing despair to overtake him, the best use of David's energy is to focus on making things better for future generations by being the one to finally break the silence.

4. **As the embodiment of this ancestor(s) in this space, place, and time, how may I atone for their wrongdoing and restore honor and balance to our family?**

   The Five of Sticks indicates that David should insist that the family deal with the abuse that has been happening for generations. He should be emotionally and spiritually prepared to hear a lot of lies and excuses and endure a whole lot of drama. David has to accept that before order there is always chaos, but he must ride the wave to help restore the balance.

5. **How should this atonement look and feel?**

   The Mother of Knives suggests that David should adopt a cool, detached, attitude as he embarks on the quest to save future generations of his family. Perhaps he could send out a group email and/or send a letter via snail mail to the heads of household with facts and statistics related to sexual abuse and its effects on families. He may suggest that the family members who are ready to deal with the issue, but maybe don't know how, should meet to discuss next steps. During that in-person or virtual meeting, he may show how others have told their story of survival and triumph and provide a list of books, video links, or free counseling resources. No matter what he decides to do, he must be unapologetic in his pursuit of the goal, and all plans should be well thought out.

6. **What will I begin to see, feel, or experience once the healing begins?**

The Big House implies he will see a dramatic shift in the family dynamic. Some people may decide to cut him off for his activism, while others may experience marvelous breakthroughs. The effect of his bravery will hit everyone like a thunderbolt either way.

LINEAGE SPREAD

We are all born to our families to learn certain lessons and contribute to the group. This spread will help you determine your mission and filial responsibilities.

1	2	3	4	5	6
7	8	9	10	11	12

1. What was I born into my maternal line to accomplish?
2. What was I born into my paternal line to accomplish?
3. How do my maternal ancestors present themselves strongly in my life?
4. How do my paternal ancestors present themselves strongly in my life?
5. What characteristic or attitude in a mate should I seek to empower my family according to my maternal-line ancestors?
6. What characteristic or attitude in a mate should I seek to empower my family according to my paternal-line ancestors?

7. What characteristics, attitudes, or lessons do I need to cultivate now to benefit my descendants?
8. What characteristics, attitudes, or lessons am I struggling with that I am unaware of that could negatively affect my descendants?
9. How can I deepen my connection to my maternal ancestors?
10. How can I deepen my connection to my paternal ancestors?
11. Am I in alignment with my maternal-line ancestral power?
12. Am I in alignment with my paternal-line ancestral power?

Sample Reading

Tiara is seeking a deeper connection with her ancestors and wants to know more information about how to facilitate that process.

Interpretation

1. **What was I born into my maternal line to accomplish?**
   Dem Bones suggests that Tiara was born into her maternal line to recognize the importance of making conscious choices. Every decision bears the seed of consequence. She must understand that though she is an individual, she is called to consider how her choices may affect the entire family long after she has passed.

2. **What was I born into my paternal line to accomplish?**

   The Four of Sticks implies that Tiara was called to establish a stable, harmonious, reliable, and happy environment for herself and any children she has.

3. **How do my maternal ancestors present themselves strongly in my life?**

   The Son of Coins indicates that Tiara has inherited her ancestors' sense of loyalty, ambition, and appreciation of nature.

4. **How do my paternal ancestors present themselves strongly in my life?**

   The Grandchildren suggests that Tiara has inherited her ancestors' creativity and their ability to endure hardship by utilizing the power of faith to make a way when the circumstances seem hopeless.

5. **What characteristic or attitude in a mate should I seek to empower my family according to my maternal-line ancestors?**

   The Ancestors card indicates that Tiara should pursue a partner who is equally passionate about healing generational curses, connecting with their ancestors, and establishing a new, stronger foundation for their bloodline as she is.

6. **What characteristic or attitude in a mate should I seek to empower my family according to my paternal-line ancestors?**

   The Ace of Baskets suggests that Tiara should only entertain partners who are ready, willing, and able to transform their dreams into a reality and inspire the best in others and who do not fear emotional intimacy. A confident person who is spiritually in tune would be the best choice.

7. **What characteristics, attitudes, or lessons do I need to cultivate now to benefit my descendants?**

   The Three of Coins implies that Tiara should focus on learning, consistent growth, the attainment of worthy goals, and the importance of teamwork.

8. **What characteristics, attitudes, or lessons am I struggling with that I am unaware of that could negatively affect my descendants?**

The Six of Knives suggests that Tiara may have a problem changing course even when she knows it's necessary because she becomes so stuck in her ways. As a result of her inability to adapt to changing circumstances, her descendants may realize that the family could have been further ahead if she had been more flexible.

9. **How can I deepen my connection to my maternal ancestors?**
    The Five of Baskets suggests that Tiara should focus more on the positive attributes of her maternal ancestors and their accomplishments instead of their failures.

10. **How can I deepen my connection to my paternal ancestors?**
    The Son of Baskets indicates that Tiara's ancestors may want her to communicate with them more or that they desire more honest communication. All genuine efforts to better understand them, their world, and why they may have perceived life the way they did (without the knee-jerk judgments and a reductive, condescending attitude) would be greatly appreciated. They want her to care more.

11. **Am I in alignment with my maternal-line ancestral power?**
    Miss Ida implies that Tiara has inherited a strong intuitive ability and the desire to use her skills to serve others from her maternal line.

12. **Am I in alignment with my paternal-line ancestral power?**
    The Eight of Coins suggests that Tiara has inherited her talents, love of learning, and a strong work ethic from her paternal line.

CAREER ADVANCEMENT SPREAD

Many people seek a promotion because it increases their prestige and paycheck, but rarely do they consider the downside. Sure, they have a fancy title and a fatter wallet, but now they have less time to connect with friends, family, and themselves. This spread will help you see the whole picture so you can consider solutions or another path altogether.

1. What is preventing me from advancing in my career?
2. What steps do I need to take to advance?
3. What will I lose by taking things to the next level?
4. What will I gain by advancing that is not currently apparent?

Sample Reading

André has been working at his job for a few years and is feeling frustrated that he isn't moving up the ladder as quickly as his colleagues and wants to know why.

Interpretation

1. **What is preventing me from advancing in my career?**
   The Father of Knives suggests that André comes across as cold, aloof, abrasive, and/or not a team player. He thinks that efficiency should be enough to get ahead, but he forgets the importance of tact and establishing the right rapport with his colleagues.

2. **What steps do I need to take to advance?**
   Pa implies that André should reevaluate his career choice or explore other positions at the company or within his field that may be a better fit for his temperament. He shouldn't permit stubbornness or fear of the unknown to prevent him from making the necessary adjustments.

3. **What will I lose by taking things to the next level?**
   The Free Man indicates that André will lose the enduring sense of dissatisfaction he's been feeling for so long.

4. **What will I gain by advancing that is not currently apparent?**
   The Two of Coins suggests that André will gain stability and a much better environment for him than he can imagine at this time. He may even make a few new friends!

CYCLE BREAKER SPREAD

Our parents are our first teachers. Our parents are also human, and, like most humans, they are complex beings with positive and negative traits. It's common for people to underestimate how their parents' negative traits have affected them, though. It's also common to play down the flaws of relatives even if we scorn strangers for doing the same things. Failure to call things what they are may be preventing you from truly understanding your fears and motivations. It could also be normalizing toxicity to any children who may witness it. This spread will help you identify how you can break negative cycles by facing any issues that you may have.

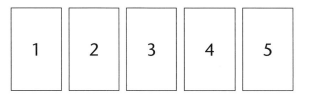

1. What is my mother's toxic trait that I try to avoid acknowledging?
2. What is my father's toxic trait that I try to avoid acknowledging?
3. How was I most affected by my mother's toxic trait?
4. How was I most affected by my father's toxic trait?
5. What is my path to resolution and healing?

Sample Reading

Gabriela is a new mother, and she is terrified of not being a good enough parent. Though her parents love her, she is conscious of the fact that they could have done a much better job. Gabriela is aware that the only way not to repeat the same mistakes with her child is to make honest self-reflection and practical action responses consistent practices.

Interpretation

1. **What is my mother's toxic trait that I try to avoid acknowledging?**
   Bishop C. H. Mason suggests that Gabriela's mother may constantly project her own moral standards and expectations onto other people.

2. **What is my father's toxic trait that I try to avoid acknowledging?**
   The Nine of Coins indicates that Gabriela's father may be materialistic, hedonistic, or selfish.

3. **How was I most affected by my mother's toxic trait?**
   The Five of Knives implies that Gabriela was most negatively affected by the tense, hostile, restrictive, and combative environment her mom created as a result of her attitude.

4. **How was I most affected by my father's toxic trait?**
   The Two of Baskets indicates that her father cared more about his relationships with people outside of the home than his own wife and children. He may have even cheated on her mother.

5. **What is my path to resolution and healing?**
   The Big Queen suggests that if Gabriela focuses on being the gentlest, most caring and nurturing mother she can be then all will be

well. She should take care not to become so obsessed with perfection that she sucks the joy out of motherhood.

POST-ARGUMENT SPREAD

When you're in the heat of an argument and often several hours afterward, it's difficult to think clearly, let alone rationally consider the other person's point of view. This spread will help you to determine the factors that caused the argument and the healthiest way to move on from here. Please do this spread once you have calmed down.

1. What is the root of the issue?
2. How did I participate in the creation of this conflict?
3. What am I misunderstanding about the issue from their perspective?
4. How is this conflict affecting my relationship with the other person?
5. What was I meant to learn from this conflict?

Sample Reading

Fabienne exploded with rage when her boyfriend, Jeff, presented her with flowers and concert tickets instead of an engagement ring on Valentine's Day. She kicked him out and refuses to accept any calls or respond to his texts. Fabienne feels her behavior was justified since they have been dating for a little more than a year, but she wants to make sure she did the right thing.

Interpretation

1. **What is the root of the issue?**

   The Four of Coins suggests that at the root of Fabienne's outburst is a fear of abandonment. She feels she must possess Jeff before she can trust him.

2. **How did I participate in the creation of this conflict?**

   The Two of Coins indicates that Fabienne may not have been as clear about her expectations and/or the timeline she expected Jeff to adhere to as she thinks.

3. **What am I misunderstanding about the issue from their perspective?**

   The Two of Sticks implies that Jeff cares for Fabienne, but he is not willing to make any hasty decisions, because the price of impulsiveness in this type of situation is way too high.

4. **How is this conflict affecting my relationship with the other person?**

   The Garden suggests that Jeff may feel that Fabienne is trying to trap him. Her behavior may end the relationship for good.

5. **What was I meant to learn from this conflict?**

   Miss Robinson indicates that Fabienne was meant to learn the value of self-restraint.

Conclusion

Polydimensionality and Rootwork in the Twenty-First Century

Hoodoo, like everything else, will continue to shift and adapt with the times. For some, that is unfortunate news, but for others it is merely a fact. The question is, What way will Rootwork change as we continue to move forward in the twenty-first century? The objective of all spiritual and religious systems is to provide guidance and comfort to their adherents. So the best way to determine the direction of any spiritual community is to keep abreast of the emotional needs and desires of average members. If the leadership of a spiritual community fails to respond to what the people want and need, then they are in danger of losing members.

For the past twenty years, various statistical agencies, social scientists, and concerned clergy have reported the increasing trend of Americans (regardless of race, ethnicity, or class) identifying themselves as "spiritual but not religious." This phrase, which is also the title of Sven Erlandson's book on the subject, usually describes a person who does not adhere to any religious dogma but still believes in, is accepting of, and/or is seeking more personalized mystical experiences.

There are innumerable reasons given for this phenomenon, including hyperindividualism, the acceptance of alternative medicine and wellness practices, commitment phobia, the proliferation of supernatural themes in popular culture, peer pressure, and an ever-increasing aversion to persons in authority.

So the recent resurgence of interest in Rootwork among younger

Foundational Black Americans is hardly a surprise, because Hoodoo's "leaders" are only responsible for their work with their own families, apprentices, students, or clients. Many Foundational Black Americans who identify as spiritual but not religious (SBNR) are relieved that they don't have to answer to any other Rootworkers and that the societal stigma against most occult practices is gone except in the most conservative parts of the country.

While the discourse surrounding SBNRs is presented as a contemporary New Age issue, I argue that (1) the term *polydimensional* is a more inclusive variant of spiritual-religious experiences than SBNR and (2) polydimensionality is not peculiar to the twentieth or twenty-first centuries but is ubiquitous throughout Western history.

Before I make my case, I want to begin by clarifying what I mean by "polydimensionality." Every religion or way of life has parameters within which exists the dimension of "thought space" that believers must inhabit and agree with to be considered a member of that group. A person who seeks knowledge and experiences beyond the boundaries of the acceptable thought space for that group is usually considered to be in great peril (spiritually, psychologically, or even physically) by other members.

This is especially true if a major tenet of that group expressly condemns cognition or participation outside the boundaries of its safe dimensional space. However, there are religions and ways of life (many of them termed *pagan, animist,* or *traditional beliefs*) today that do not demand exclusive intellectual and spiritual control over their adherents. Members of many of these communities are free to explore and participate in rites and rituals without fear of meta or social condemnation, yet they are indeed religious.

Therefore, I find the term SBNR applicable only for former or unconventional believers of Abrahamic faiths or any other religions/ ways of life that generally discourage intellectual or spiritual exploration outside of their realm. It is because of the implication that all religions have the same boundaries (which they do not) that I refer to all people who feel comfortable beyond a single spiritual/religious paradigm as having a polydimensional consciousness. This does not mean that all polydimensionals are polytheistic or animist, but perhaps polydimensionals have other means by which to determine whether certain information or practices are right for them.

They might consult their own conscience, priests/elders from their traditions, divination, or any number of other means. Once Christianity became dominant in the Western world, polydimensionals were forced to study certain subjects solitarily while others formed clubs or highly organized secret societies with like-minded people to avoid persecution. Occasionally, the occult becomes fashionable to the masses, and it is socially acceptable to host séances, tell fortunes, use Ouija boards, become a devotee of an Eastern guru, and so on. During these times life is significantly easier for consistent polydimensionals to blend in with the trendy crowd.

We know Hoodoo has survived the oppression and persecutions of yesteryear by remaining relatively unknown to outsiders. Today, younger generations have no problem discussing Hoodoo and openly identifying themselves as practitioners. This has the positive effect of destigmatizing and normalizing Hoodoo, but it has also caused many in the community to become anxious and afraid that Rootwork will be exploited by other ethnic groups as a result.

Cultural appropriation and identity in general have been hot topics in the twenty-first century, which is not a surprise since the questioning of social boundaries and living authentically, a.k.a. "keeping it real," were major talking points during the latter half of the twentieth century. For many people, living moral, authentic lives includes what they perceive as the ethical harvesting and dissemination of spiritual information by going directly to the community. To others, that means choosing not to engage in any occult practices outside the realm of one's bloodline ancestors and/or not teaching anyone outside of their race/ethnic group.

So what are the factors involved in the construction of a polydimensional identity? The answer is prismatic and could be approached through a multitude of disciplines, but I have attempted to distill it to four *c*'s: commerce, conquest, calcification, and curiosity.

Commerce and conquest affect culture as it relates to the verbal and nonverbal transmission of ideas. In the case of the latter, the material culture of a people communicates information, which is then reinterpreted through the lens of the observant population, whomever they may be. Humans have always traded goods with or have been dominated by foreign populations whether the outsiders were from another country, race, ethnic group, or tribe. While it is possible to contain or suppress the process of cultural diffusion as a result of commerce or conquest, it is impossible to avoid it altogether for the buyer, the seller, the conqueror, or the conquered.

Calcification and curiosity relate to the shift in consciousness that inevitably causes groups to become dissatisfied with the status quo, begin to question its validity, and consider other possibilities. This cycle is most often discussed and expected in the realms of politics and fashion, but somehow people tend to forget that religions are not exempt from the cycle of life.

On this point, American philosopher John Herman Randall Jr said, "Men are prone to regard the body of their beliefs as they do the hills to which they lift up their eyes, as fixed and immutable, and all departures therefrom, as in the very nature of the case absurd. Or they treat them as coins of tested gold, always able to pass current in any land or age."

In terms of religion, it is my observation that most people are not entirely dissatisfied with their cosmologies as much as they are dissatisfied with calcified interpretations of them that inhibits movement.

Throughout history, failure by religious authorities to recognize the beginnings of calcification and reconsider the changing needs of their constituents breeds a desire for something more, which inevitably leads to their downfall. However, there is a lengthy exploratory stage between desire and dissolution that is fueled by the curiosity developed after the status quo's validity came into question. If during this phase there is access to novel ideas, then there is a tendency for people to supplement any perceived deficiencies of the native faith and its rituals by syncretizing the exotic concepts with one's own. Initially, those who do this may experience harsh criticism, oppression, or worse from representative authorities/adherents of the native and appropriated faiths.

Yet it all begins with tenacious curiosity and what I call an "immortal jellyfish consciousness," which is a nonconformity that seeks to solve and resolve rather than to destroy or be destroyed. For example, the ancient Egyptian religion was able to adapt quite well despite centuries of foreign invasions and a constant influx of immigrants. It worked because whenever they encountered new ideas that inspired the populace, they incorporated it into their corpus without ever destroying their foundational beliefs. However, it must be noted that the contemporary obsession with purity, with regard to race, religion, sex, and so on, began much later in history, so they felt in no way indecisive, inauthentic, or hypocritical about having multiple creation stories, adding new deities, and so forth. The reason being that the ancient Egyptians focused on the abstract lessons, the meanings of symbols, and personages instead of literal or historical facts.

It is also important for me to emphasize that the desire for supplementation is not being judged here as either positive or negative. It is merely a common reaction to dissatisfaction with the status quo, the factors of which are dependent on the conditions in which that population find themselves, the influences that surround them, and the resources available to them.

The Mediterranean in the first century CE was as racially and culturally diverse as New York or London is today. Like modern cities, there were significant portions of the population that were first-, second-, or third-generation immigrants who continued to serve the pantheons of their homelands. This undoubtedly had an influence on Mediterranean people who interacted with newcomers on a daily basis either as tradesman, artists, fortune-tellers, or domestic slaves. Thus, it was during this era that adherents of African and Asiatic mystery cults reached their height.

However, in Rome the gods of the state continued to be propagated by all (as was mandated by the government), and it was normal for people to belong to several priesthoods or cults simultaneously. That more or less mimics the contemporary situation for millions of polydimensionals who may still celebrate state religious holidays (Christmas, Hanukkah, Eid, etc.) or participate in the rites/rituals of state-recognized religions (baptisms, fasting, etc.), but in their private, everyday lives, their spiritual journey may take them to the mysteries of distant lands.

For the contemporary polydimensional, propagating "state gods" is not compulsory as it was for their ancient counterparts but doing so may be convenient for many. By officially claiming membership in a socially acceptable religion or way of life, they may avoid ostracism, punishment, or the loss of credibility. People who are unconcerned about the loss associated with their polydimensionality fail to mention their multifaceted belief system either because they don't have the desire to provide an explanation, or they don't thoroughly understand it themselves.

Unlike ancient times, the modern world is harsh on those perceived to be hypocrites and demands that people choose one deity or the other. The modern world simply does not have within its consciousness the possibility of henotheism, or logic in the form of complementary propositions. Instead, polydimensionals are accused of having questionable ethics or are dismissed as confused and undisciplined. Adding to the troubles for polydimensionals is the current appropriation discourse that might make them fearful of appearing insensitive to other cultures, making them reluctant to seek tutelage or advice from religious or spiritual leaders who possess knowledge they may be seeking.

Today we live in a world that is more connected, more economically interdependent and homogenized than at any point in documented history. Therefore, polydimensionality is not only common, but its proliferation is inevitable. Thus, I argue, the general discourse surrounding religion in the twenty-first century is largely deficient and should transcend simplistic classifications of belief as more people adhere to multiple ideologies simultaneously because of enhanced cultural diffusion. It will be very interesting to see how Hoodoo and its practitioners come to terms with all of these factors in the years ahead.

Bibliography

Andrews, E. D. "The Dance in Shaker Ritual." *Dance Index* 1, no. 4 (1942).

Baer, Hans A. "Toward a Systematic Typology of Black Folk Healers." *Phylon* 43 (1982).

Butterworth, Andrew. "African Christianity Thrived, Long Before White Men Arrived." Africa.TheGospelCoalition (website), November 16, 2022.

Croft, Wayne E. *A History of the Black Baptist Church*. Prussia, Pa.: Judson Press, 2020.

Cullina, William. *Wildflowers: A Guide to Growing and Propagating Native Flowers of the United States and Canada*. New York: Houghton Mifflin, 2000.

Dearden, Taylor. "Similarities of the Native American Medicine Wheel and the African Cosmogram." Medium (website), February 9, 2018.

Diekelmann, John. *Natural Landscaping: Designing with Native Plant Communities*. Madison: University of Wisconsin Press, 2002.

Dogo, Sefinatu Aliyu. "The Nigerian Patriarchy: When and How." *Cultural and Religious Studies* 2, no. 5 (Sept.–Oct. 2014): 263–75.

Dulken, Danielle. "A Black Kingdom in Postbellum Appalachia." Scalawag Magazine (website), September 9, 2019.

Fillmore, Charles. *Metaphysical Bible Dictionary*. Wellington, New Zealand: Unity Books, 1995.

Hartz, Paula. *Native American Religions*. New York: Facts on File, Inc., 2004.

Krochmal, Arnold. *A Guide to Medicinal Plants of Appalachia*. USDA Forest Service, 1969.

Malinowski, Sharon. *The Gale Encyclopedia of Native American Tribes*. Farmington Hills, Mich.: Gale/Cengage Learning, 1998.

McCulloh, J. H. *Researches, Philosophical and Antiquarian, Concerning the Aboriginal History of America*. Baltimore, Md.: Fielding Lucas, Jr., 1829.

Mellichamp, Larry. *Native Plants of the Southeast*. Portland, Oreg: Timber Press, 2014.

Paul, Heike. *The Myths That Made America*. Bielefeld, Germany: Transcript-Verlag, 2014.

Perry, Imani. *South to America: A Journey Below the Mason-Dixon to Understand the Soul of a Nation*. New York: Ecco, 2022.

Puckett, Niles Newbell. *Minor Charms and Cures of the Southern Negroes*. Whitefish Mo.: Kessinger Publishing, LLC, 2010.

Raines, Ben. "One of America's Great Wildernesses Is Being Destroyed Bit by Bit, in a Silent Massacre." *Los Angeles Times,* November 29, 2020.

Reed, Roy. "Blacks in South Struggle to Keep the Little Land They Have Left." *New York Times,* December 7, 1972.

Salami, Minna. "There Were No Matriarchies in Precolonial Africa." MsAfropolitan (website), June 4, 2012.

Stewart, Dianne M. "The Wedding Tradition of Jumping the Broom Didn't Actually Derive from Africa." Oprah Daily (website), June 25, 2021.

Swanton, John R. *The Indians of the Southeastern United States*. Washington, D.C.: Smithsonian, 1979.

Tallamy, Douglas. *Bringing Nature Home: How You Can Sustain Wildlife with Native Plants*. Portland, Oreg.: Timber Press, 2007.

Wallace, Cathy. "Native American Burial Rituals." BillionGraves (website), 2021.

Index

Page numbers in *italics* refer to illustrations.